Modern Clinical Hypnosis for Habit Control

Modern Clinical Hypnosis for Habit Control

Charles M. Citrenbaum, Ph.D.
Mark E. King, Ph.D.
William I. Cohen, M.D.

W • W • NORTON & COMPANY
New York   *London*

Published simultaneously in Canada by Penguin Books Canada Ltd,
2801 John Street, Markham, Ontario L3R 1B4

Printed in the United States of America

First Edition

Library of Congress Cataloging in Publication Data

Citrenbaum, Charles.
  Modern clinical hypnosis for habit control.

  Bibliography: p.
  Includes index.
  1. Appetite disorders – Treatment.   2. Cigarette
habit – Treatment.   3. Alcoholism – Treatment.
4. Hypnotism – Therapeutic use.   I. King, Mark.
II. Cohen, William I.   [DNLM: 1. Habits. 2. Hypnosis.
WM 415 C581m]
RC552.A72C58   1985   616.86′06512   85-3019

ISBN 0-393-70003-8

W. W. Norton & Company, Inc., 500 Fifth Avenue, New York, N.Y. 10110

W. W. Norton & Company Ltd., 37 Great Russell Street, London WC1B 3NU

1 2 3 4 5 6 7 8 9 0

And the journey continues:
The Jewel is always there as its beautiful and deeper Character
  emerges,
The Aura grows in intensity to the wonderment and amazement
  of all,
The Rainbow spreads his shining light in search of his true call,
The Katydid will surely bring more happiness you know,
And the Deer and the Parrot and P. S. at its end really started
  a great show.

C. M. C.

To Virginia Bonnie
  — I travel, I don't know where
  — The journey ends, I don't know when
  — I whistle on the way, often losing the tune
  — How strange and wonderful that you walk the road with me.

M. E. K.

To Mark King, Charlie Citrenbaum, Lin Ehrenpreis and, especially, Terry Boots:
  Can you possibly know the magnitude of my gratitude?

W. I. C.

CONTENTS

INTRODUCTION

THIS IS A BOOK about the use of modern clinical hypnosis for the treatment of habit disorders. By modern clinical hypnosis, we refer to hypnosis as it was articulated by Milton H. Erickson, M.D. This hypnosis is permissive, respectful, and often indirect and metaphoric. It is also understood as an extension of everyday communication, not a separate "be all and end all" tool. We use it as part of a treatment package in conjunction with other strategic therapy approaches that will be elaborated on in this text.

A habit disorder can be considered any unhealthy repetitive behavior that phenomenologically speaking is out of the person's control. More specifically, however, we are referring to habit disorders as those behaviors relating to the intake of food or other chemicals, such as tobacco and alcohol. For the purpose of coherence, we have limited our examples to problems concerning food, cigarettes, and alcohol. It is our experience that the greatest number of persons coming to a professional who uses clinical hypnosis will be concerned with these issues. The techniques discussed herein are applicable (with some modifications) to most habit disorders. For example, many of the techniques can be used directly as presented for nail biting, hair pulling and gambling. Some other habit disorders, such as heroin or cocaine dependency, will require additional strategies.

This is not a book on how to do clinical hypnosis. We do not believe this skill can be learned from reading a text. This is, rather, a book about the specific treatment of habit disorders for those health professionals who are already skilled in the use of clinical hypnosis.

There are three major difficulties that challenged us as we

wrote this text and that may do the same for many of the readers. First and most importantly, the organization of this material is necessarily arbitrary. It does not lend itself to clear categorization. For example, some of the indirect techniques (Chapter 4) can also be used or understood as direct techniques (Chapter 5) or vice versa. There is a strong interaction between what we refer to as belief systems in Chapter 1 and techniques discussed in detail throughout the rest of the book. We hope that we have presented the material in such a way that the reader will have a sense of the total picture by the end of the text. The chapters depend on each other and we suggest that they be read in the order presented and within the same general time frame.

A second difficulty for us was in dealing with the problem of language. Language is a left brain activity and a cumbersome tool to use when trying to describe hypnotic communication which involves right brain functioning. As Nietzsche wrote, "That which we have words for, we've already gone beyond. Words are for the ordinary, the mundane. In every spoken word there is a grain of contempt by the speaker."

The language of hypnosis is so precise, with every word important, and yet so loose, leaving many gaps for the patient's unconscious to fill in. The communication depends not only on words, but on tonal shifts, pauses, body shifts by the therapist, etc. Imagine the difficulty of being limited to words and a few still photos as our only means of communicating with you.

We have purposely chosen to write a relatively short book because we believe that the bottom line is that you need to use these techniques in a way that is suited for your own style of therapy. As you do this, we suggest that you keep your sensory channels open and continue to modify all the procedures to get the best results for each patient. We could have made this text three or four times longer but we believe it would have mired you in detail that would have actually inhibited your use of these techniques. For those of you who hunger for more, at the end of the book we include a bibliography that will be a helpful guide. Also, many of these techniques are discussed from a slightly different perspective in a previous book by two of the authors, *Irresistible Communication: Creative Skills for the*

Health Professional (King, Novik, and Citrenbaum, 1983); some readers may want to refer to that text.

A third difficulty had to do with remembering some of our sources. Collectively we have attended an almost uncountable number of workshops, conferences and classes. Listing all the books we have read in this volume would require cutting down too many trees—even if we could remember them all. In Chapter 1 we discuss the major influences on our thinking about this topic, but there are many other teachers and writers to whom we would like to say a collective "thank you." Many of their specific ideas have not been identified as theirs because we have so completely internalized them ourselves.

We would also like to take this opportunity to thank Susan Barrows, our knowledgeable editor from W. W. Norton and Company, for her belief in our project and her valuable help along the way. A thanks also to Linda Helm for her help in the development of the manuscript. A very special thanks to The Division of Professional and Public Education at the Sheppard Pratt Hospital in Baltimore, Maryland, especially to the former Director, Priscilla Tainter, as well as to Pat Mitchell and Sylvia Nudler. This organization and staff have for many years sponsored our hypnosis workshops around the country and their support has been critical in the development of our ideas.

Last of all, a slanted tip of our Organ Stop Pizza hats to the American Tobacco Institute, The Potato Chip and Snack Food Council of America, and the Association of American Brewers and Distillers. Without these groups this book would not be possible or even necessary.

Modern Clinical Hypnosis for Habit Control

CHAPTER 1

BELIEF SYSTEMS

Argue for your limitations, and sure enough they're yours.

Bach, 1977

SORRY, BUT THIS IS NOT a book about how to do clinical hypnosis. If you don't already possess that skill or training, we have to tell you that you probably need to invest much more than just the price of this book. We don't believe anyone can be trained in the science and art of hypnosis without spending the time and energy necessary to find and study with people who are already skilled in such techniques. This is a book intended for people who already know how to use clinical hypnosis in their profession, and would like to read about some effective strategies for dealing with habit disorders. In order for you to understand the techniques we use for specific disorders, we first need to share with you our underlying belief system about human nature, psychology, health professionals, and clinical hypnosis.

About five years ago one of our daughters, who was six years old at the time, came out of her bedroom one night to see her father practicing hypnosis with a friend in the living room. She said, "Daddy, what's this hypnosis anyway?" He said, "Shana, it's a way to help people believe different things." She said, "What do you mean?" He said, "Well, for example, this person believes he can't do something, and because he believes it, he can't do it. I'm attempting to help him believe something differently." She looked at her dad and said, "You mean you can do whatever you believe you can do?" and her dad said, "Almost." And she said, "You mean, you can't do what you believe you can't do?" and her dad said, "Definitely." And she just looked

3

at him and said, "Huh, I don't understand," and he said, "Well, Shana, you're too young to understand." About every six or eight months for the next five years, she would ask her dad, "What's this hypnosis stuff that you teach anyway?" and he would always respond with an explanation similar to the above, and she would always end up not understanding. About a year ago, she came home excited from fifth grade science class one day and said, "Dad, guess what I just learned? I learned that a bee's body is much too heavy for its wings and the bee shouldn't be able to fly, but the bee doesn't know it, so it can fly!" Her dad looked at her and smiled and said, "Shana, now you understand what hypnosis is all about."

Nutritionists tell us that we are what we eat, but psychologically speaking, we are what we believe. This is as true for the health professional as it is for the patient. We cannot overestimate the importance of understanding your own belief system and how it affects your work and of understanding your patient's belief system and how it affects the particular symptoms that bring him or her into your office.

We hold this truth to be self-evident — we don't have any truth to tell you. We are not particularly bothered by this fact because in our professions we deal with realities, not truths. Finding out the "truth" about something is the job of philosophers or preachers. Even though at times we like to think of ourselves as either or both, the fact is that as health professionals what we need to understand is what is *real* (what is believed by our patients), however that corresponds to what will inevitably be unknown metaphysical facts. It is beyond the scope of this book to elaborate in detail on this blatant existential-phenomenological approach to life. For those who want more detail, we refer you to Valle and King (1978). Suffice it to say that we define reality as anyone's understanding of the world. Jean Piaget has demonstrated that very young children do not understand that objects exist outside of their perception. Consequently, if you want to understand the terror of a young child whose parent has just left, you need not inquire about the truth (that is, the parent is just in the next room); rather, you need to understand the cognitive functioning of the child, and therefore, the child's reality (that is, the parent is gone).

Paul Watzlawick, in his brilliant book, *The Language of Change* (1978), discusses the phenomenon this way. Patients come into your office believing as if the world operates a certain way. That particular belief system is not very functional to them; that's why they are coming to you for help. Your job, then, is to help them believe as if the world operated a different way. However, as you do this it is important to keep in mind that neither the way the patients originally believed nor the new system of believing that you helped them to develop has special validity. From a philosophical viewpoint, both are probably flawed. The difference is that the new strategy, if it is effective, should be one that helps the patient live a more comfortable and enjoyable life, while the old belief system is one that caused the patient pain and suffering.

Sometimes it is necessary to help patients change their belief system. For example, patients who believe they have absolutely no control over their eating patterns need to establish a new belief system which says that they do have some control over their eating patterns. Sometimes, however, it is not necessary to change the belief system of patients; all that is needed is to help them understand their present belief system in a slightly different way. An example of this would be a smoker who comes in and tells you how stubborn he or she is, believing that stubbornness will make it difficult for him or her to break the smoking habit. The job of the professional, in that case, is to let the patient know how helpful stubbornness will be in his or her effort to stop smoking—because, after all, smoking is such a difficult habit to break that it takes a really stubborn person to "stubbornly" stop smoking.

While most of this book deals with the belief systems of patients and how to use or change them for patients' benefit, we begin by asking you to examine *your* beliefs about the nature of therapeutic change in general, and specifically about clinical hypnosis.

Each of you is a professional communicator, in that your ability to work with patients depends not only on your knowledge of psychodynamics or medicine but also on your ability to communicate that knowledge effectively with patients. If you are an effective communicator, you will communicate all your belief systems about therapeutic change to your patients and even beyond that to their families and friends. One of us had a patient enter the office, look him right in the eye and say, "I'm an oral character so treating me will be difficult." The therapist immediately went into trance, which is what we always do when we don't understand what's going on. This patient's husband had been in psychoanalysis for five years and the analyst was able not only to communicate his belief system about human behavior and change to the husband, but even to convey it to the patient's family. So at this time we are going to ask you to think about what you believe about the nature of change. Unfortunately, many schools of psychotherapy tell you that real personal change comes with great difficulty and is usually slow. If you do believe this, you will communicate it to the patient, and then you shouldn't be surprised when you get these so-called "resistant" patients who don't like coming to therapy. Who wants to deal with something that's painful and takes a long time to do? Our own belief about therapeutic change is that *human be-*

ings can change most patterns of behavior relatively rapidly and that change can be quite interesting and often even fun. We believe this, as best we can we live it, and in every way possible we communicate it to our patients.

Having already begun, what we would like to do now is communicate to you our belief systems about therapeutic change and hypnosis, so that you can understand the underlying philosophy that grounds the rest of the book. We begin by giving credit to the professionals who have been most influential in shaping our thinking. The first person that we want to mention is Milton H. Erickson, M.D., "the father of modern clinicial hypnosis." Erickson is the person most responsible for making hypnosis respectable again in the medical field. His ideas – and in a small way even his personality – permeate this book. Erickson was a person who was so far ahead of his time that he was clearly misunderstood and under-appreciated while he was alive. However, it seems that he has also been misunderstood in his newfound fame over the last decade. There are many books recently published claiming to use "the Ericksonian approach"; yet Erickson disavowed this label often during his life. He used to say that he took a different and personal approach for each patient, that there was no "Ericksonian approach," and that no one should attempt to copy him or misunderstand him in that way. Also, if you have not been fortunate enough to meet Erickson or extensively study his videotaped work, then you might have the misimpression from reading many of the recent books about him that all his work was in metaphor or riddle. While he was the master at indirect communication and helped us appreciate its value and strength, he often worked quite directly with people, in terms of both inductions and specific strategies to deal with their problems.

Nietzsche, the philosopher, once wrote to one of his students, "You could honor me as your teacher by ceasing to be my student" (1968a). We think we could all honor Milton Erickson by not engaging in competition to see who can do the best Milton Erickson imitation, but by taking his work and using it in our own particular idiosyncratic ways to help patients. While we have been strongly influenced by Erickson and clearly appreciate his values, this book should not be read as an attempt to replicate or present his work.

Two men whose ideas and techniques have been particularly helpful to our work are Richard Bandler and John Grinder, the founders of a school of psychology called "Neurolinguistic Programming." Richard and John are particularly skilled observers who studied the therapeutic techniques of Milton Erickson, Virginia Satir and others, and were able to elaborate and explicate what they did so well. Dr. Erickson once told us that he learned a lot about his own work from Bandler and Grinder. These men, particularly, taught us the effective learning strategy of finding people who are very good at what they are doing and modeling or studying these people in great detail.

Theoretically, this work is also heavily influenced by Paul Watzlawick, whose books, along with Bandler and Grinder's and Milton Erickson's, are listed in the back of this text. We believe him to be probably the leading theoretician today in the field of psychotherapy. In the same manner, the insights and techniques of Jay Haley have also been especially influential for the three of us.

THERAPEUTIC STRATEGIES

There are four particular techniques or strategies for change that are important both for the use of clinical hypnosis and for therapy independent of the use of clinical hypnosis. The first of these, known as *pacing*, is so critical to effective therapeutic work that we have devoted an entire chapter just to its elaboration (see Chapter 2 for a detailed discussion).

The second technique that is critically important and often overlooked in the teaching of therapeutic skills is *the skill of being an acute observer.* Perhaps this was Erickson's greatest skill. We remember our first moment with him, when he was wheeled into the room by his wife Betty. We know he had not seen us come in—he was feeling ill that day and was late. He looked around the room, gave us his famous stare, and then said, "Who in this room walks differently from the rest of you?" All of us—including the person he was speaking about—looked around puzzled. After a few moments he pointed to one woman and said, "Would you walk across the room?" She did. When she returned to her place he said to her, "How long have you been a dancer?" He was able to tell from the body posture of this woman as she sat in the room that something was different, and as he watched her walk across the room he knew she was professionally trained in dancing. This experience and many of the remarkable stories told about Erickson are really explained by his incredibly sensitive ability to observe the smallest detail about a change in a person. We think of our own training in psychology and medicine. The teachers considered accurate observation as the ability to objectively observe behavior of the patient instead of making theoretical interpretations about it, and we now realize how elementary this training was. Erickson, as well as Bandler and Grinder, helped us learn to observe skin tone changes, breathing pattern changes, slight shifts in the body, etc., as being important variables in understanding what is happening in the hypnotic process.

The third technique is commonly referred to as *utilization of behaviors*, and we should add to that *utilization of belief systems*. Dr. Erickson believed that every patient who entered his office brought gifts for use in treatment. Many of these gifts aren't commonly used by therapists because they are artificially labeled as symptoms; then therapists feel that their job is to get rid of them, never realizing that the "symptoms" could be used in that process.

Perhaps the most elegant example of utilization is given by Jay Haley in *Uncommon Therapy* (1973). A young man who was hospitalized in Massachussets as a paranoid schizophrenic believed himself to be Jesus Christ. The staff complained that they couldn't get him to participate in any of the therapeutic situations on the ward or in the hospital, that all he would do was pontificate all day long. After all, you wouldn't catch Jesus Christ in group therapy. Erickson, who was working at the hospital at the time, was assigned this case. Before he even met the patient, there were a number of things he knew about this man and was able to use that to his advantage. Erickson walked up to the man the first time he met him and said, "I heard you used to be a carpenter." Of course, the man had to say, "Yes." Then Erickson said, "And I heard you like to help people," and again the man had to agree. Erickson said, "Good," handing him a hammer, "We have construction on the charity wing over there in the hospital and we need your help." In a few moments this man was in what we now would call occupational therapy or milieu therapy, with a group of hard hats who didn't really care who he thought he was, as long as he could learn to be quiet and hammer the nails in straight. Soon the man was released from the hospital, able to function in the outside world.

Not many of us will have such elegant examples in our caseload; however, some common examples will demonstrate the usefulness of this technique, in terms of both psychotherapy in general and hypnosis in particular. One of the authors, when he was just learning about hypnosis, was hypnotizing a friend of his in his home. At the time he lived in a house with a number of people, although he thought no one was home at the time. When he began the induction he was startled to hear the shower in the next room go on. Instead of despairing at this distraction, he utilized the noise, proceeding with the induction as follows: "and as you hear the shower in the room next door, you can begin to think of warm, soothing water running down your back; and with each drop of water going down your back, you can begin to let yourself go more and more." The noise of the shower became an auditory stimulus, an integral part of the induction.

Another simple example of the utilization of a belief system was given earlier in this chapter, when we talked about taking a patient's belief that he is stubborn and utilizing that in the treatment. We congratulate all our patients who believe they are stubborn, telling them that we are going to need their stubbornness in order to effectively work on their problem because it takes a stubborn person to give up whatever habit they happen to be working on at the time. So whether the gift is an outside distraction, a belief system, or a series of behaviors that we label as pathological, it can be used in the patient's best interest by a skilled practitioner.

The fourth specific strategy for clinical effectiveness has to do with maintaining *flexibility as a clinician*. Most of us learn particular ways to behave with patients. These behaviors usually reflect the theoretical orientation of the graduate or professional school we attend. Obviously these behaviors work some of the time or we would never use them. The problem is that, when the behavior we usually use does not work, many of us just use the same behavior again, longer and louder. When we finally use it as long and loud as we possibly can and it *still* does not work, we get into name calling. If our ego strength is particularly good, we end up calling the patient a name; the psychotherapy example of this is the notion of the "resistant" patient. If our ego strength is lower, we just call ourselves names and think of ourselves as ineffective clinicians. The strategy of flexibility is elaborated by Bandler and Grinder as "The Law of Requisite Variety" (1979). This principle says that you work with a patient in the way you sense is best and you keep your sensory channels open. If that way is working, then obviously you continue with whatever small adjustments are needed; but if that particular method is not working, then you try something else. We agree with Bandler and Grinder that if you have more flexibility or more variety than the patient, in the long run you will be able to get the patient to make the change he or she needs, and you'll never see in your practice such a thing as a "resistant" patient.

This notion calls upon us to reassess our notion of professionalism. We have very strong feelings about this topic, and in the workshops we teach around the country we spend a great deal of time on it. Simply put, to us the professional is someone who gets the job done well, and an amateur is one who does not. There are no other clear distinctions. Professionalism doesn't have to do with the way you dress, or with your office, or with any other trappings. A humorous story about Milton Erickson relates that when he was first beginning his practice in Michigan, a doctoral student in another department was doing a dissertation on professional offices. He walked into Erickson's office and noticed a card table and some uncomfortable chairs. The student said to him, almost apologetically, that, even though he was doing research and was not supposed to be commenting, he could not help but say that this just was not the way a professional office was supposed to be. Erickson looked him in the eye and said, "Yes, but I am here!"

Too many of us have inflexible guidelines about the notion of professionalism that hinder our effectiveness with many of our patients. One of the most common but often unspoken assumptions is that health professionals are supposed to be nice. While we agree that it is nice to be nice in those situations when we can be pleasant to people, it is important to remember that patients can drown in chicken soup. Some patients require "a kick in the ass," and a professional who does not have the ability to give it is less effective than one who has the flexibility to be both nice and "hard," as the situation requires. This is particularly true with certain kinds of habit disorders, such as drug and alcohol abuse, where we believe that the professional often must take a very hard line with the patient.

Following the rule of doing what works allows — sometimes even demands — personal flexibility. Sometimes we do work in our offices; sometimes we do work in a park outside. Sometimes we wear suits and ties when we work with patients, and sometimes we wear T-shirts. It is important to remember that all of our behaviors are purposeful. We use our flexibility as far as the limits will allow but without violating a few essential ethical guidelines, such as not having sex with patients. We suggest that all therapists reexamine their ethical guidelines to make sure they really have to do with ethics and are not just a disguise to protect them from their own inflexibility.

In summary, we believe that a therapist who can get in pace with patients (see Chapter 2), has good observation skills, knows how to utilize what the patient brings into the office, and has a wide range of behaviors to choose from when deciding how to deal with each patient will have a good start toward being an extremely effective change agent, both hypnotically and in psychotherapy or medicine in general.

THE ISSUE OF CONTROL

Control is a very ambiguous, controversial and difficult issue to deal with in a patient-professional relationship. Obviously, the ultimate goal of the treatment is to give patients more control over their life and to allow them to experience themselves less as victims of habit. However, paradoxically, we believe the professional needs to do this by initially taking control of the situation. Many of the techniques we discuss in this book are very controlling maneuvers. For example, if a patient calls up and insists upon an immediate appointment, we will make him wait a week, even if we have time on the calendar. Now, we understand this is a debatable tactic and there are other professionals who would take the opposite point of view. However, we believe that in order for professionals to maneuver or manipulate the situation to their patients' advantage, they must be in control.

Democracy is not a very effective way to run a professional practice. As students in the '60s, we too often sat through classes where the "humanistic" thing was for the teacher not to be in charge. So teachers would sit cross-legged in front of a room and say, "What do you want to do today?" In most cases what we did was nothing. Whether in a classroom or a medical practice or psychotherapy, we believe the professional must be in control.

Now, many people shy away from the word manipulation. We openly admit that we manipulate patients all the time. After all, physical therapists manipulate the patient, and nothing is wrong with it. Manipulation, in fact, is a responsible part of their job. They restore the muscular-skeletal system by manipulating, exercising and strengthening damaged or weakened muscles, recreating a balance so the patient can be mobile. Physical therapists do not manipulate or take control of the person's life or spirit by deciding what the patient should do with the restored mobility. They are only responsible for manipulating the patient's muscles so that the muscles can again be under control of the patient. The therapist working with habit control issues has a similar responsibility. The temporary assumption of control and manipulation by the health professional has as its goal the restoration of the patient's ability to totally control his or her own life.

Control, in and of itself, has no value. Whether it is good or bad depends on the intention of the clinician. If the clinician is working for the best interests of the patient, then it is his or her job to control, manipulate, or do whatever is necessary to make the patient better. Being a "nice guy" but ineffective is of no value to the patient. This might be the basis for a friendship, but not for a therapeutic pay-as-you-go relationship. We even lie to patients, and we believe that is OK too as long as it is done for the purpose of helping them.* <u>If we make up a story about a friend with the intention of conveying a metaphoric message to the patient to help him or her deal with a problem, then we believe it is not only OK but also obligatory.</u> We believe our obligation as health professionals is to do the best we can for the patient. Of course, if we tell a lie for the purpose of getting more money from a patient or of luring a patient into bed, then that is unethical. Again, ethics applies to the intention of the act, not to the act itself. This book is a clear example. If every case history were made up, that would have no bearing on the value of this book. If, after reading this book, you are able to work more effectively with patients, then you have gotten your money's worth. If, on the other hand, every word we say in this book is true and when you put it down you're still no better off in your profession, then you've wasted your money, no matter how honest or sincere our effort has been.

Now, this is a very difficult thing for many clinicians to deal with, simply because we are saying that professional skills are measurable, not by intentions, not by particular techniques, but by success. This is particularly true with habit control, because the goals of treatment are usually quite clear-cut; the patient will or will not stop smoking, will or will not lose weight, will or will not give up alcohol abuse, etc. We have met many professionals who like to fool themselves into thinking they are quite competent. Even though their patients do not get better, they talk about their ethical stances, their fancy techniques, the size of their offices, etc. We believe that the only thing that matters is that patients get better; if they do, no matter how you maneuvered them or what you've told them, within the bounds

---

*In our workshops, we now refer to this behavior as creating "therapeutic fictions," which seems more acceptable to some. A rose by any other name does seem to smell differently.

of reason, you've done a good job. If they don't get better, you've done a poor job no matter what you've done.

OUR BELIEFS ABOUT WEIGHT CONTROL, SMOKING AND ALCOHOL ABUSE

In this book we will be discussing in detail three particular habits which bring a lot of people to the doctor's or therapist's office. These are problems of weight control, smoking, and alcohol abuse. There are many other habits that we will not be discussing. Among these are other substance abuse dependencies, gambling, nail biting, hair pulling, and thumb sucking. We believe the principles are applicable to all of these habits, but in order to concentrate and be more specific in our description of the techniques, we are limiting ourselves to the three habits that in our experience affect the largest percentage of the population looking for help.

Let us look for a moment at the people who come into therapy for these problems. First of all, of the habits mentioned, the largest population consists of people concerned with weight control. Weight control is a billion dollar business in this country today, and hypnotists get more than their fair share. The majority of patients seeking treatment for weight control are women. This does not mean that there are more medically obese women than men; rather, because of social pressures and concern about appearance, proportionately more women come into therapy to deal with this problem. The majority of men who come for weight control have medical problems and are referred, sometimes even pushed, by their family physician. In our experience, smokers break down about evenly in terms of sex and slightly more men than women seek treatment for alcohol problems.

Interestingly, people who come for habit control often have other issues. Unfortunately, in this country today it is still more socially acceptable to see a therapist for a problem with smoking or overeating than for interpersonal or psychodynamic reasons. Anyone who deals with this population must understand that it is not uncommon for a male to come in to work on smoking, and, after finding out that he can trust the therapist and be comfortable, say, "Oh, by the way, I haven't had sex with my wife for two years either." We will discuss this issue in more detail later.

We would like to explain why we refer to these disorders as habits as opposed to addictions. As we will discuss in detail in Chapter 7, we do not believe that the physiological addiction involved in many habits is very severe. Addiction has the connotation of being out of the person's control, and we believe this is not the case. Therefore, we talk to our patients about "behaviors" or "habit disorders" as opposed to "addictions." In dealing with habit disorders, the whole issue of physical versus psychological addictions is a red herring. It is just a rerun of the old mind-body split that should have been put away a long time ago philosophically. We believe clearly in the dialectical relationship between the mind and the body. The two are inseparable; they have never existed without each other, except in the state of coma. Suffice it to say we believe René Descartes was wrong centuries ago when he postulated the difference between a subject and an object, between the seen and the seer, and we do not plan to spend 50 pages dealing with a topic that psychology and medicine should have put away a long time ago. For a more detailed discussion of our belief system around this issue, we refer you to Chapter 1 of Valle and King (1978), where it is discussed in some detail.

HYPNOSIS

This is a book intended for clinicians who are already familiar with basic techniques of clinical hypnosis. We make no claim or attempt to teach the basic skills of induction here. What we do want to discuss here are some of our beliefs about hypnosis, hypnotizability, levels of trance, ethics, etc., to be used as a background for the rest of the text.

First of all, let us focus on two ethical issues, one of which is very simple and clear-cut to us, and the other of which is much more complex and unclear. The first ethical rule is that hypnosis is a tool to be used within a specialty in which you are already trained. While each of the three of us is skilled at helping people with pain control, none of us would attempt to fill a cavity just because we could help a patient numb his or her mouth. This is because we are not trained in dentistry. Likewise, we do not expect a dentist who is skilled in clinical hypnosis for relaxation or pain control to be doing psychotherapy, which he or she is not trained to do. We stated earlier that many times people come in for what seems like help with a simple habit and end up dealing with many more complex issues. Also, habits themselves are quite complex and, as you'll see in some of our more clinical chapters, understanding the dynamics and payoffs behind them is critically important. We are assuming that our readers have training and skills not only in clinical hypnosis, but also in a particular profession in which they are using clinical hypnosis. We never refer to ourselves as hypnotists, but rather as psychologists or physicians.

The more complex ethical issue has to do with how hypnosis is presented to the patient in terms of its "magical" ability. We do not believe hypnosis is magic and do not like to falsely present it as such. It is an effective clinical tool that helps many people (some almost magically, some less so) – and that doesn't help some people at all. However, we also believe strongly in the notion of self-fulfilling prophecy. We believe that if we present it as a powerful, almost magical, tool, then that increases the probability of its having positively powerful effects. Thus, we have a dilemma. Actually, this is so complex that we do not have an answer, other than to say that we try to pace (see Chapter 2) the belief system of the patient as she presents it to us during the initial phone contact and initial interview. Often we tell people that hypnosis is not magic, that it is something to supplement their willpower, that it will help them get over the hump or the point where they failed previously. On the other hand, some people come in with magical expectations, often referred by physicians who say, "This treatment and this particular person will help you." And to a certain degree we support this belief system because, again, of our strong belief in the importance of self-fulfilling prophecy. Along this line, we also understand that some of the positive effect of hypnosis is probably a placebo effect. People are told that this is the treatment that will help, that this is the person who will help, and we certainly do not want to negate that effect. In summary, all we can say is that we recognize this is a complex issue. We do not have a simple answer to this problem and suggest that clinicians consider it strongly and probably adjust their approach, depending upon clinical intuition, as they begin to work with each new patient. An obvious question to ask and answer here is, "What is hypnosis?" An answer is, "We really don't know." We could say it is an altered state of consciousness, but that evades the issue in a sense. What we do know about hypnosis is how effectively it works and how it can be used. In a way, it is like electroconvulsive therapy for depression. We know what it works for, we know certain variations of techniques (such as bipolar or unipolar electrode placement), but we do not know exactly why it works. The same is true for hypnosis. With the advanced technology that is coming of age in brain research, we expect that the answer will be scientifically forthcoming within the decade. We await it as anxiously as you probably do. In the meantime there are some notions we have about hypnosis that we want to share with you.

First, let us consider the sticky question of susceptibility or hypnotizability. There have been debates in the literature; for two good summary articles that together present all points of view we suggest you read Weitzenhoffer (1980) and Barber (1980). It is our belief that anybody who has an attention span longer than a couple of minutes can be hypnotized. The clinical question to be asked has to do with motivation. We have run across people in workshops who have been tested by various susceptibility scales and told that they have almost no susceptibility. Yet, we found many of them quite easy subjects when hypnosis was used appropriately. We are quite convinced that if a so-called unhypnotizable subject was to fall down in front of us and twist his ankle painfully, one of us could say, "Listen to me for one minute and you'll be out of this pain," and we would have a quite susceptible subject.

The laboratory studies measuring susceptibility essentially introduce an experimental factor into the situation. Subjects have no motivation to be hypnotized; they are simply laboratory subjects. Also, in order to insure proper experimental controls, most of the studies use "canned" inductions that are not individually geared to the subject. The problem with the notion of hypnotizability is that it gives the clinician too much of an excuse. Instead of using the flexibility and utilization of behavior that we talked about earlier, hypnotists will often try one or two approaches that they are comfortable with; if those do not work they just label the subject "nonsusceptible" and that ends the matter.

It is our conviction that every person who comes into our office can, in some way, use trance work. It is our job to find the appropriate time and method for that trance work to take place. While this may seem like a radical statement, we utterly reject the notion of nonsusceptibility. There are patients who, for reasons of their own, will not go into a trance. A common example is a person literally pushed by his or her family and doctor to stop smoking, who really does not want to stop smoking and who believes that if he goes into a trance he will stop smoking. This is a nonsusceptible subject – not because he cannot roll his eyes a certain way or because he has a certain personality structure, but simply because he is more motivated *not* to go into a trance than to go into a trance. The clinical problem is that the screening procedure was not good enough to eliminate him in the first place (see Chapter 8).

Another notion that is talked about in the literature quite frequently has to do with level or depth of trance. In our own clinical experience there have been only very rare instances when such distinctions are useful. While it is clear that there are different levels of trance that seem idiosyncratic to the person involved, we have seen miraculous change take place in subjects who have been in such light trances that an unskilled observer would not even call it a trance state. We have also observed people who have gone into deep, almost sleep-like trances, and yet not improved. So while we confess to clearly observing different levels of trance, our own clinical experience has found no correlation between the so-called depth of trance and clinical effectiveness.

Now the first thing to remember about trance is that it is a very natural phenomenon, rather than a unique experience that is produced only in the health professional's office. Almost every person has natural trance experiences every day. At the end of this chapter we will demonstrate how we educate patients about trance as a way of preparing them for hypnosis.

There are two types of trance experiences, which we refer to as "little h hypnosis" and "big H hypnosis." Big H hypnosis is the formally induced trance, usually used in a clinical setting. Little h hypnosis is this natural phenomenon that we talk about. A good example of little h hypnosis is that momentary daze or trance that one goes in after being confused. In this sense one of the great hypnotists of all times may have been the late comedienne Gracie Allen. The whole point of her character was to constantly miss the point about anything, and so to follow her crazy logic, one literally needed to go into a quick, brief, what we call little h trance. Consider the following sequence:

Gracie: "When are you going to marry your boyfriend, Edna?"
Edna: "I don't know if we will, because we're having a disagreement."
Gracie: "What's it about?"
Edna: "My boyfriend thinks that his wife should work after she gets married."
Gracie: "Why, I agree with him."
Edna: "Well, how come?"
Gracie: "Because you wouldn't want her bothering you around the house, especially after you and Eddie just got married."

We can understand trance better if we have some knowledge of the functions of the left and right sides of the brain or, as psychologists say metaphorically, the conscious and the unconscious mind. The left side of the brain, or what we refer to as the conscious mind, is in charge of our analytical process. It controls all language, does mathematics, etc. The right side of the brain has no natural language in the linguistic sense. It functions using sensory experience such as visual imagery and has a profound effect on human behavior. Metaphorically we refer to this as the unconscious part of the mind. Now at this point we run into a linguistic problem, because we are trying to explain the functioning of something that does not use language to function. We are essentially using left brain concepts to explain the functioning of the right brain. Or we might say that we are trying to make you conscious of what really is not conscious.

One of the best ways to understand this phenomenon is to study the research on those individuals who have had a commissurotomy, an operation that severs the connection between the two sides of the brain. This operation has been performed on approximately 200 people in the past 15 years, usually to prevent uncontrollable seizures in the subjects. These individuals may be some of the most interesting individuals in the whole world to study because they literally have two functioning brains that are totally independent and in fact have no way to communicate with each other.

Studies of these individuals all show the powerful influence that the right brain, or unconscious, has on our behavior, even though we are not aware of it. In a typical study (Sperry, 1968), the subject was asked to fix his eyes to a dot in the middle of a TV screen. On the right side of the dot was the word "pink." Now that was seen by the right visual field, which connects to the left side of the brain. On the other side of the screen was the word "banana," which was seen by the left visual field connecting to the right side of the brain. The subject was then given a choice of ten colored pencils to do with what he pleased. What the subject did was pick up the pink pencil and draw a banana. When he was asked about this, he could explain that he picked a pink pencil because he saw the word pink on the screen, since the part of him that is in charge of his language was from the left side of the brain and thus understood the concept of pink. However, when asked why he had drawn that banana, he had no idea and would make up reasons such as, "Well, I picked it up with the left hand and a banana is easy to draw because the lines all go down." The fact is that we know that his right brain, or unconscious, was clearly influenced towards the concept of banana, enough so as to affect his behavior and have him draw a banana, and yet he was totally unaware of it. When asked why he drew a banana, the subject developed his own theory as to why he thought he was drawing a banana, totally unaware of the unconscious influence.

There have been literally hundreds of studies with patients like the one just described, demonstrating the powerful influence of messages that go to the right side of the brain and the total lack of conscious awareness the subject has about those influences. For a more detailed review of all this literature we refer you to Springer and Deutsch (1981). Our understanding of hypnosis is that trance is a state of consciousness wherein the subject is open to receiving messages by the unconscious or right side of the brain. A good hypnotic induction and good hypnotic work will stimulate that side of the brain and will thus have a powerful influence on the person, oftentimes out of his awareness. The most important advantage of working out of a person's awareness is that it allows the subject to suspend critical judgments from the left side of the brain (such as beliefs that he cannot possibly do something or that the world couldn't possibly be one way when she is sure it is another way). Instead they have the ability to form new frames of reference for certain behaviors or situations. Put differently, by using the unconscious mind or right side of the brain, the health professional is able to bypass any conscious resistance that the patient has. The person is influenced to alter behavior in ways that will be healthier without engaging in the unnecessary dialogue that often accompanies analytic therapy.

In the modern hypnotic approach developed by Dr. Erickson, insight is not useful; in fact, it is often detrimental to treatment. People often use insight or left brain conversation with themselves or their therapist or physician to continue the same excuses for not getting better. The alternative approach is to influence a behavior change in the direction of health and allow the new attitudes to develop naturally as the behavior changes, rather than the other way around. This is why most hypnotists, influenced by Dr. Erickson and his colleagues, regularly use forgetting messages as part of the trance procedure (see Chapter 4). The less the patient can remember about the session, the more effective the work probably will be.

We often teach that there are three main functions of trance

To resist hypnosis, the patient recognizes its existence. There can be no resistance to the non-existent, & its existence implies the possibility (Milton E.)

1. work. The first is the suspension of critical judgment that was
2. just mentioned. The second is that trance slows down the physiological processes of people and then allows them, both at a conscious and unconscious level, to really concentrate on the task at hand, to access experiences from the right side of the brain, and to understand their problem differently with the left side of the brain. The third major function of trance is that it sets
3. up a really nice cooperative relationship between the clinician and the patient. This relationship facilitates good clinical work both in and out of hypnosis. This is done in two ways which are elaborated on in great detail in our earlier book, *Irresistible Communication* (King, Novik, and Citrenbaum, 1983).

In that book we discuss the two major ways to communicate with patients so that you never see this phenomenon known as "resistance." The first way is to set up a situation where the patient cannot fail. Whatever she does is correct. The metaphor we use for this is that we shoot the arrow in the air and whatever it hits we call the target. While this may seem like some hocus pocus, the fact is that after a short while the patient feels that he or she cannot lose, relaxes, and gets involved in the task at hand. Again, let us share an example of this from the work of Dr. Milton Erickson. He would often ask subjects in the trance state for an arm levitation. In a high percentage of cases, he would receive the behavior he requested; however, when he didn't, he would just look at the subject and say, "Good, you're already in a deeper trance than I thought possible yet." In this way he defined the non-levitation behavior as indicative of an even deeper trance than he had thought possible so early in the trance work. In doing so, he created a therapeutic double bind. Whatever the person did, he was cooperating and doing just fine. If he levitated his arm, of course, this was some proof to him that he was in trance and clearly in a cooperative relationship with the hypnotist. But if he did not it was not defined as noncooperation or nontrance behavior; rather, it was defined as a deep trance.

Again, believing in the power of self-fulfilling prophecy, we know that if you tell people they are cooperating, they, in fact, will begin to believe it and within a short time will be in a totally cooperative relationship with you. This type of work takes all the test anxiety away from patients because they never fail the test; whatever they do is fine. In doing formal trance inductions we often ask people to imagine numbers on a blackboard and count backwards from a 100 to zero, but we give the direction in such a way as to let them know that it will probably get harder and harder to see and say the numbers (which we know is an inevitability), and yet that they should *try* to go to zero. Again, this is another example of a therapeutic double bind where patients cannot fail. If the numbers get harder and harder to say and see, and patients don't get to zero, then they are doing exactly what we predicted they would do, and they will define themselves as good trance subjects. Those who do struggle down from 100 to zero are also cooperating, since we asked them to "try" to do that. We thank them and give them the next direction. Either way, we set up a situation where there is no struggle between the therapist and the patient, and eventually we expect to get the patient's total cooperation.

Another guideline for getting totally cooperative patients is to avoid telling them how they are feeling. We assume that everyone who comes into therapy, especially for habit disorders, has a part that does not want to give up the habit. People would not pay the kind of money we charge and spend time coming to our office to give up smoking if there was not a little part of them that wanted to hang on to smoking (otherwise they would throw the cigarettes in the trash can and go about their life). A mistake many hypnotists make is to tell people what they feel, which allows this little resistant part of the person to take over. If you make the mistake of utilizing a trance induction that tells people that they are feeling more and more relaxed as they feel this warm wave going up their body, then all they need to do is create some tension in some part of their body for one of two things to happen. Either they discredit you because you are telling them they are relaxed when they are not, or they blame themselves and think that they have failed at hypnosis. The fact is that if you want your patients to relax, all you need to do is to have them focus their attention long enough on anything. What we often do is have people pay attention to different parts of their body, one part at a time, noticing the difference in feelings for each part of the body as they compare how it feels when they inhale to how it feels when they exhale. (Of course, we are always pacing the individual, to be discussed in detail in Chapter 2. This means that we use the word "inhale" as the person is inhaling, and we use the word "exhale" as the person is exhaling, etc.) In that way we set up a fail-safe situation, because as long as individuals are willing to go along to the point of following directions, they cannot possibly lose, since we never tell them how they feel. We know that if we do what we do long enough, we will get the result we want without any chance of failure.

Once again, by setting up situations where people cannot be wrong and by not telling them how they feel but reporting back behaviors only (almost as a human biofeedback machine), we set up this cooperative relationship in which patients are concentrating both at a conscious and unconscious level, and where they have allowed themselves to be open to new frames of reference by suspending critical judgments. These are the keys to success in clinical hypnosis.

Unless there is a medical emergency involved, we usually talk to the subject about trance before we actually begin an induction. Even though this varies from person to person based on the initial belief system, we thought, as a good way to summarize some points in this chapter, we would provide a transcript of a very typical introductory discussion.

> Now, Susan, I would like to tell you a little about hypnosis before we begin. The first thing I want to tell you is that trance is a very natural phenomenon. You've gone into trances many times, even if you haven't been formally hypnotized. For example, I bet you could remember times when you have driven your car down a familiar street or highway, and gotten so mesmerized thinking about a conversation you were about to have with someone, or going over one you just had, or listening to the stereo in the car, that your conscious mind got occupied and you didn't even

notice some of the signposts you usually see along the way, or maybe a restaurant, and yet part of you was driving that car safely because under such conditions the person hardly ever misses the turn off the turnpike or crashes into the car in front of her. Well, that part of you that was driving the car is what I call the unconscious and that whole experience really is a trance experience. Or, maybe you could remember another time when you were at a show or a concert or a speech, where the content of what you were observing was so entrancing that when it was over you couldn't believe it. You looked at your watch because it only seemed like 10 or 15 minutes, and were surprised to find out it was an hour and a half; you didn't even remember moving a muscle during the performance. That also was a trance.

In fact, trance is so natural that many times when people first have a trance experience in this office, they are disappointed by the experience, and in fact feel like they've failed. I remember the first time I had a formal trance experience 15 years ago. It was late one Thursday afternoon after a long day's work, and I could remember sitting there hearing everything the person was saying, not feeling sleepy or unaware, and I was sure that I was failing at the experience and I was very angry at myself. Then the hypnotist suggested that I imagine helium balloons attached to my wrists, and as I imagined that, I saw my hand rising. But you know what, Susan? I knew that I was putting my hand up, and I knew that I could put it down anytime I wanted to, except it just seemed reasonable to cooperate – after all, that's why I was there. (*This, of course, is also a subtle message requesting cooperation from the patient.*) Well, it wasn't until after my hand stayed up there for about an hour and 15 minutes, Susan, that I thought to myself, "Huh, something unusual must be happening."

Now again, as you experience trance for the first

time, hopefully after a while you will allow yourself to get more and more comfortable, but you won't experience the dramatic out-of-this-world feeling that many people believe hypnosis is; however, there are signs of trance that I could help you discover to let you know that you are having a somewhat extraordinary experience.

Now, the second thing Susan, that I like to talk to every patient about, has to do with whether or not you can go into a trance. You know, Susan, almost everyone who comes into my office, whether a well-known surgeon, a scrub lady from the same hospital, or anywhere in between in the social hierarchy, all seem to have the same fear that maybe they can't do it. And I'd like to let you know that I know you can do it. In fact, Susan, I am convinced that anyone who has an I.Q. of 80, and I'll assume that includes you, can go into a trance. There are just a number of ways to do it, and when you hear this idea of people not being able to go into a trance it is usually some bad hypnotists who only know one way to do it and if that way doesn't work, they say the patient can't go into a trance. Let me take the pressure off you, Susan, by letting you know that I consider it my job to help you go into a trance. Now I don't know how fast you'll go into your trance. Some people do it immediately the first five or 10 minutes. Some people take most of the first session; some people don't do it until the second session when we've tried the fourth or fifth way. But I want you to know that I know you can go into a trance, that I will take the responsibility for that happening, so that you can relax and just enjoy this experience. Now Susan, it's clear if somebody came in and said "I bet you can't put me in a trance," then they would be right and I wouldn't even try, but for someone like you, coming here and paying money and wanting to take care of this problem of yours, the motivation to work is clearly there, and once again

I want to tell you I have no doubts about your ability.

The last thing I want to tell you, Susan, about trance, has to do with the notion of control. (*At this time I usually take out an inch and a half long 20 gauge needle and hold it in front of the subject, which in itself is trance inducer since so many people are afraid of needles.*) Now you see this needle? When we go around the country teaching hypnosis to physicians, and we are working on pain control, we take this needle and stick it in the back of people's hands, in one side and back out the other side, through that vein. Now, if people can allow themselves to be very comfortable during that experience, what that reminds me of is the kind of self-control we read about when the Eastern yogas walk on hot coals or do things like that. <u>Maybe you have learned how to ride a bike at one time</u>, and if you did, probably somebody helped you, maybe your dad or a brother or a sister, by <u>holding the side of the bike for a few minutes</u> while you <u>got your balance and walking along with you</u>, until they let go. When they let go you were the one in control the whole time. The person on the side was just a <u>teacher or a helper.</u> And rather than seeing myself in control of you, which I am not, <u>I see myself as helping you to learn the ultimate in self-control.</u>

Now, oftentimes Susan, when people come in here, control is an issue because you may have seen or heard about people on stages, doing silly things like barking like a dog, or opening your eyes and thinking you are naked on stage, something of that nature. Let me explain that to you. What stage hypnotists get is what is known as a volunteer effect. That is, what they do is pick a person who clearly would like to be up there, not one who is being volunteered by a spouse. When that person has a drink or two in them in a night club and goes on stage with the magician and stage hypnotist, they understand that they are going up there to make an ass of themselves, and it's not really because they want to make an ass of themselves, but rather because they want to go back and tell their friends that they were hypnotized and what a neat experience that was. That's why you get the kind of phenomenon you see in nightclubs. Now Susan, I think that I am probably a better hypnotist than any nightclub stage hypnotist you will find, and yet I doubt that I can get anyone to come into my office and bark like a dog or jump around like a chicken. That would be a degrading, uncalled for experience for them, and I doubt that I could get people to co-operate in that manner. People often ask me, "What happens if I have a heart attack while deeply in a trance?" And I say, "I have no doubt you'll open your eyes, alert yourself, go to the telephone, dial 911, and since we are here at the University of Pittsburgh they'll put you on hold for a few minutes," (*this usually gets a laugh out of the patient*). I also have no doubt that even in the middle of the deepest trance if you smelled smoke you would open your eyes and notice what is going on and do what you needed to do for yourself. The point is, that you are totally in control the entire time during this experience, and I think you'll find that out very soon.

So, once again Susan, as a summary, this is a very natural experience that may, in fact, even disappoint you at first, that it's not more mystical; however, when you see the nice results you'll get you won't be disappointed at all. It is something that I know you could do, I have no doubt about your ability to go into a trance and do this kind of work, and it's a situation in which you are really learning the ultimate in self-control. You will never really be under my control in any way. Now Susan, do you have any questions you would like to ask me about hypnosis or about myself before we start?

One final note to end this chapter: Clinical hypnosis can be a very powerful tool. We have already discussed the therapist's need to be in charge of the whole therapeutic process. We have also mentioned that, even though the patient is actually learning the ultimate in self-control by experiencing hypnosis, there are many fantasies that people come in with about being controlled through hypnosis. The one way to diffuse much of the tension around these control issues is through the use of humor. Dr. Milton Erickson was a very powerful man. Even in his old age, when he was sick and confined to a wheelchair, being with him had an element of fear to it because it was almost like he could read your mind (this was because of his acute observation skills). But Dr. Erickson also had a marvelous sense of humor. He never seemed to take himself or the situation he was in too seriously.

Many of our patients have worked hard to solve their problems; they have taken their situation so seriously that they have become almost immobilized. It does not help for the professional to have a notion of "serious" professionalism that feeds right into the patient's immobilization. A relaxed, humorous atmosphere is probably the best clinical environment for healthy, productive work, as well as for teaching and learning.

 "You're only here for a short while, so have a few laughs and don't take things so seriously — especially yourself."

— Mark Twain

CHAPTER 2

PACING

MANY ADDICTIVE PATIENTS can be metaphorically viewed as stuck on a cliff above a treacherous ravine not knowing where to turn or what to do. The clinician on the safe side of the ravine can call to the patient and plead that he come over, but it is likely that the patient will continue to feel scared and confused and will not budge. Instead, the clinician can go over to the patient, take him or her by the hand and lead him to a safer, healthier place. This is how we characterize the concept of pacing or leading, which is basic to the modern hypnotic approach. Pacing means meeting the patient at his or her reality of the world so that the patient can then be led to healthier and more satisfying realities.

The two main forms of pacing are verbal and nonverbal.

VERBAL PACING

Here is a clinical example of verbal pacing in an eating disorder case. A young woman entered one of our offices for the first time. She was obese and unkempt, stated that she was a "horrible mess" and that "people can't stand to be near me." While a typical compassionate response might have been to try to reassure her that things really weren't that bad, a more helpful clinical stance was to pace her as follows: "Yes, you are a horrible mess and I don't know how long I can stand to be around you, so let's do what's necessary to change things." This woman said, "Thank you for hearing me. I'm glad I've found an honest therapist." In this example, the clinician paced what the patient said, even using similar words, and then began to lead her to a better place.

Using verbal pacing, the communicator mentions experiences,

either past or present, which are undeniable to the listener, and then adds a suggestion that will usually be accepted. Milton Erickson sometimes referred to this form of communication as use of the "yes set." Early in his work, Erickson (Erickson, Rossi, and Rossi, 1976) found that if subjects were presented with a series of statements that would in all likelihood be answered in the affirmative, then there would be a higher probability of accepting the next statement. This is very similar to contingency suggestions to be discussed in more detail in Chapter 6. Here is an example of typical hypnotic communication using truisms to form a "yes set": "You're looking at this page, your eyes are aware of the words that are printed on it, your mind is following the thoughts, and you may be curious about just how much your professional effectiveness will increase by reading this book." A way to conceptualize the above statement is *pace, pace, pace* and *lead*. Lead statements suggesting trance could, of course, constitute the basis of a hypnotic trance induction (e.g., "As you continue to read, let yourself drift into a nice trance").

Another way to understand the concept of pacing is that it involves communication which is always "on the mark" in terms of the patient's experience. Therefore, it will tend to be accepted by the patient; this enhances the cooperative nature of the therapeutic relationship. Hypnosis can be conceptualized as two persons pacing or being in sync with each other. In such situations, the person in control (hopefully the clinician) can lead the patient to other realities. As was mentioned in Chapter 1, effective hypnotic communication is always undeniable in that it accurately reflects the patient's experience. An effective hypnotist tends to engage only in communication that is "fail-safe," thus pacing the patient. To further illustrate, here is a partial transcript from a hypnotic session:

> And now your eyes are closed. And you can hear my voice, and you're breathing in (*said when the patient breathes in*), and out (*when the patient breathes out*). And you may be aware of that fluttering of your eyelids, and they can continue to do that or stop only as soon as they're ready to. And the sound of my

voice, the hum of the air conditioner next to you, the loud backfire outside (*as the patient flinches upon hearing that*), the sound of my voice. And it's nice to tell you that your conscious mind can attend to anything now, since your unconscious will hear everything I say. And you're breathing in, and out, and as you hear that phone ringing, you can let yourself go into your trance and you may not even notice it a whole lot just yet.

The above hypnotic communication nicely paced the patient's ongoing experience and was fail-safe. There are two other important things to notice about this pattern. First, during this induction there was a loud noise that could have been experienced by both the patient and the therapist as an interruption. Using the concept of pacing, every sensation that the subject becomes aware of can be commented on, thereby becoming part of the trance induction rather than an interruption. Secondly, even if the patient had not become aware of a trance experience, the "just yet" at the end of the sentence still prevents this from being "wrong" and also sets up a self-fulfilling prophecy of trance in the near future.

The reader may recognize that pacing is a form of utilization discussed in Chapter 1. We do not fight with the patient by telling him or her what the experience is in a way that could lead to a disagreement. Instead, we communicate our understanding and acceptance of the patient's realities. This alliance with the patient helps him or her to trust, enhances the cooperative nature of the relationship, and facilitates leading the patient to healthier patterns.

REPRESENTATIONAL SYSTEMS

A helpful and interesting way to effectively pace patients is through knowing and using the representational systems of experiencing. This concept has been elaborated upon in great detail by Bandler and Grinder (1975).

Please imagine this: You're at a beautiful beach on a sunny

day. There are seagulls, sand, and waves splashing against the
beach. Now, how did you experience that? Some readers might
be aware primarily of nice images of the beach scene that they
saw in their mind. Others may have mainly heard the associated
sounds, for example, of seagulls calling and surf splashing. Still
other readers may be mainly in touch with good feelings – the
warm sun on their skin, the soft sand or the nice breeze. Of
course, many of you may have experienced the beach using all
three of the sensory modalities described – visual, auditory and
kinesthetic. However, we all tend to use one of these systems
in a preferred or predominant way, a process that is for most
people usually at unconscious levels. The preferred modality is
called a person's *primary representational* (or *rep*) *system*. The
other two senses – smell or olfactory and taste or gustatory –
are not as predominant in human experience as the visual,
auditory and kinesthetic senses, but are certainly important in
many animal species. The point here is that determining and
utilizing the patient's primary rep system increase the clinician's
ability to pace that patient effectively. The two ways to determine a patient's primary representational system are 1) listening
to the predicates that are used in sentences and 2) observing eye
scanning patterns.

Use of Predicates

By listening to the verbs, adverbs and adjectives that a patient uses, the clinician can determine the patient's primary rep
system and then match his own predicate usage to the patient's.
When the therapist matches the patient's predicates, the patient
is better able to understand the therapist's communication and,
especially at intuitive levels, to know that the therapist understands him or her.

Patients whose primary representational system is visual will
often use words such as *look, see, clear, picture, bright* or *dark*.
Those who are primarily kinesthetic will use *feel, heavy, light,
pressure, grasp* or *hold*. People who are auditory will have sentences replete with such words as *hear, say to myself, talking,
sounds like, tune in*, etc.

To illustrate, let us first study an example of communication that is poor because the therapist is not pacing the patient's predicate usage:

Patient: "Doctor, I tell myself all the time that I better stop drinking, but I just can't do it. I came here to hear what you have to say."
Doctor: "I guess you're feeling upset about this, huh?"
Patient: "Well, I've thought about it a lot, and I've talked to friends and now it's time to hear you out."
Doctor: "So how do you feel about your drinking?"
Patient: "How do I feel? What do you mean by that?"
Doctor: "Well, you know. What's your gut level reaction to all this?"
Patient: "Doctor, I don't understand. I was hoping you'd say something to me that would ring a bell."

Of course, the above patient's primary representational system was auditory but this kind-hearted clinician was trying to move the patient to a "feeling" level – perhaps what he was taught to do in graduate or professional school. He was not pacing the patient's experience. In such a scenario, the doctor above might spend six months or a year teaching the patient to "be in touch with feelings" so that therapy could then proceed. By matching predicates initially, communication and treatment would have been greatly facilitated.

In contrast, here is an example of effective clinical communication that matches the patient's preferred representational system, in this case, visual.

Patient: "I've been smoking for 40 years. A smoke has helped me to get through a lot. I just can't see myself without a cigarette."
Doctor: "I understand, but you can take a look at that scene later. First, let's look at the entire picture."
Patient: "What picture do you mean?"
Doctor: "I mean like how cigarettes have been your companion in many ways and helped you out over the years."

Patient: "Yes. I'm glad you understand that perspective. You seem like the kind of professional who can shed some light on all of this."

Finally, to pace the reader whose primary representational system is kinesthetic, here is another example of effective communication:

Patient: "Doctor, I feel terrible carrying around all this extra weight."
Doctor: "I'm sure it's quite a burden to shoulder."
Patient: "It sure is. But I don't feel strong enough to diet without some help."
Doctor: "I'm happy to help out. You'll be standing on your own two feet soon."

In each of the above examples, the primary representational system of the patient was obvious. However, in some cases, it is much more difficult to ascertain the patient's preferred system, or the clinician may be communicating with two or more persons with different primary systems. In such situations, the clinician can use two or three of the rep systems, or use neutral verbs (e.g., "*I understand* what you mean"). Other neutral verbs are *think, consider, aware, experience*, etc.

Eye Scan

Please take a few moments and answer this question: <u>How many doors are there, inside and out, in your apartment or home?</u>
Having answered that question, you may be aware that while you were solving that problem, <u>your eyes went up and to the left.</u> For some of you, you may have been aware of just staring straight ahead, perhaps looking in a daze. During that time, it is very likely that your pupils dilated. The point here is that in order to answer the question of how many doors are in your home it was necessary for you to <u>visualize.</u> You had to see the outside and the inside of your home, images that you have seen

before. Also, in order to visualize those images that you have seen, your eyes had to go up and to the left, or stare straight ahead while your pupils dilated. This process is called *eye scan* and is associated with neurological hook-ups that exist in all of us. Right-handed and most left-handed people move their eyes up and to the left or stare straight ahead while their pupils dilate as they access *visual tapes* (sometimes referred to as visual eidetic) – that is, to see things in the mind that have been seen before.

Now, please imagine this: a green elephant with wings, and tires instead of legs. For most people, accessing this image necessitates a scan of the eyes up and to the right. Such visualizing is called *visual constructive*, that is, constructing a visual image that hasn't been seen before.

When most people access sounds that they have heard, their eyes go down and to the left. This type of experience has been called *auditory tapes.* Sometimes a person's eyes will shift back and forth across a horizontal plane; this is indicative of an auditory experience also. It usually means that in his or her mind the person is talking to himself or to somebody else. If you ask someone to be in touch with how he feels about a loved one, that person's eyes will quickly scan down and to the right to access to this kinesthetic experience. We often remember this by the mnemonic "feels right."

Eye scan occurs unconsciously for most of us. In fact, you may have already noticed that it is quite difficult to be consciously aware of this process. Observing eye scan can sometimes be useful to the clinician in revealing what representational system the patient has accessed at that moment. For example, a clinician might notice a very reticent patient staring off into space, primarily up into the left. At that point, the clinician can pace that patient's experience by saying, "I wonder what you see up there?" This has occurred several times in some of our clinical work, and in such cases the patient typically says, "How did you know I saw something up there?" If the patient is holding his head with his left hand in a "telephone posture" and looking down and to his left, then an appropriate communication to pace this situation might be, "I wonder if you can tell me what you're saying to yourself right now?" Such a question has a much higher probability of eliciting some responsiveness from the patient than other communication, since it paces that patient's experience. It is also a way to short-circuit any censoring the patient may do of mental processes. When the patient responds to a question such as "What are you thinking?" he has to translate from "seeing" or "hearing" or "feeling" in his mind to the generic concept of "thinking," and this gives him time to "filter" what he says to the therapist. When you pace the patient by asking him what he is seeing, hearing, or feeling, the reaction time will be quicker and the verbal responses a more accurate representation of his mental processes.

For most people, observing eye scan in a reliable way takes hours of practice. However, the time and effort are well spent since this skill adds greatly to their power and effectiveness as communicators.

NONVERBAL PACING

Another way to pace a patient is to simulate or mirror the person's nonverbal behavior. Imagine two people entranced in a conversation with each other. As they sit or stand facing each other, *they unconsciously mirror* each other's bodily posture and gestures. It is very likely that they are also breathing at the same rate. If one person shifts position in some way, it is likely that the other will follow that lead and shift in a similar fashion.

Nonverbal pacing consists of mirroring the other person's bodily posture and gestures as well as breathing in and out at the same rate. It must, however, be done in such a way that the patient does not become consciously aware of the process. For example, if the patient shifts his or her body, the therapist casually moves a few moments later to mirror the patient's posture. Nonverbal pacing also includes speaking with a similar tone and tempo as the other person. For example, if a patient comes in acting tense and edgy, therapy will be more effective if the clinician initially engages in bodily movements similar to the patient's and also speaks in a tense manner. If the patient is shifting his body, the clinician can do the same. If the patient folds his hands, the clinician can slowly and subtly move his hands to that same position. If the patient crosses his legs, then the clinician can do the same. If the patient's breathing is rapid, then the clinician may speed up his own breathing. Once in pace with the patient, the clinician can slow down his own bodily movements and thus help the patient to do the same. If a patient comes into the therapist's office and refuses to sit down, it would be a "non-pace" to continue sitting and to repeatedly suggest to the patient that he or she sit. As is often the case with clinical behaviors which are a non-pace, the above situation would just generate even more patient resistance. Instead, we would suggest that the clinician stand up with the patient. Once in pace with the patient, the clinician can slowly sit down and the patient should follow that lead.

As already mentioned, people who communicate with each other will usually be in pace with one another quite unconsciously and *keeping pacing behaviors out of the patient's conscious awareness will add to their power.* The patient's unconscious will perceive that the therapist is a person who accepts his behavior and is similar or familiar to him. This acceptance will generate trust and enable the patient to follow the therapist's lead to other realities.

This nonverbal pacing can sometimes be amazingly powerful. For example, at our hypnosis workshops we have a 75% success rate at nonverbally pacing and then leading a volunteer to sit in our "trance" chair at the beginning of the workshop. Before the workshop we will select a participant, admittedly one who looks receptive initially to our communication, and write down a description of that person. Then we will nonverbally pace that person's breathing and posture and then lead him or her with our eyes to the trance chair before asking for a volunteer. When we are successful at this, we are always very careful to express our appreciation to that workshop participant, especially to his or her unconscious, for the communication and the cooperation.

A good way to test whether you are in pace with the patient is to modify your behaviors and then observe whether the patient follows your lead. For example, after some initial clinical communication in which you are nonverbally pacing the patient's bodily positions and gestures, shift your feet and see whether the patient does the same. If not, it probably means that you need to do some more pacing. Some of you may already be aware that a very effective way to induce hypnotic trance is to be in pace with the patient consciously and then to lead the patient into trance by letting yourself go into trance. If you are in pace initially, then the patient should follow that lead. This technique may be combined with a verbal hypnotic communication to help lead the patient into trance.

In some situations pacing nonverbal behavior is not recommended. One is when the behavior in question might be obnoxious or disturbing to the patient. For example, certain pathological motor movements like facial tics or bodily ataxias would, of course, not usually be paced by the clinician. We have found, however, that after some initial verbal pacing even disturbing motor behaviors can be nonverbally paced. In one case, a man with severe arthritis was helped to learn to move more comfortably when the therapist first paced his tense and stiff movements and then slowly let go of some of the bodily tension, which helped the patient to do the same. Eventually the patient learned to let go of such bodily tension and stress quickly, thereby relieving his pain.

Generally speaking, effective clinical communication or hypnosis is enhanced by behaviors which pace, verbally and nonverbally, the behavior or experience of the patient. This, of course, entails the flexibility or requisite variety to vary clinical communication accordingly. Thus, the expert hypnotist might at times talk in a slight Southern drawl to a patient reared in Georgia, use some street slang in communicating to an inner-city alcoholic patient, or tell some metaphors about sports to an athletically inclined person. We observe and listen carefully to patients for any data that we might later utilize for a better pace. As already mentioned, it is best to keep your pacing behaviors subtle and out of the patient's conscious awareness. This will prevent the patient's generating resistance because of a perception that the clinician is mocking him or acting in a condescending way.

As you pace the patient, it is always important to remember

that the final goal is not to make yourself a mirror image of the patient, but, rather, to quickly build up the trust required to allow you to *lead* the patient into new, healthier behaviors. Pacing is a technique, not an outcome. The ideal outcome is also not to have the patient become a mirror image of the therapist. A good TV repairman fixes your television, but does not require that you watch certain shows.

In closing, let us offer an illustration from the clinical practice of one of the authors which nicely illustrates the use of verbal and nonverbal pacing and parallels the elegant communication style that was so often used by Milton Erickson.

The therapist was sitting in his office when the patient, a 15-year-old boy, angrily entered the room. The teenager walked back and forth, protesting that he had been forced to come by his parents. The therapist immediately stood up, pranced back and forth with the patient and loudly stated, "How dare your parents! Who do they think they are, forcing me to see you? They've got some nerve." They continued to jointly admonish the parents for several minutes. Finally, the therapist began to slow down as he stated that he and the patient were going to have to talk about how the teenager would be able to deal with the parents. The teenager agreed as he sat down with the therapist and treatment began.

CHAPTER 3

ANCHORING

HAVE YOU EVER noticed what happens when, driving your car along the Interstate, you hear a siren and in your rearview mirror you see a police car flashing lights? Do you get a sinking feeling in the pit of your stomach or feel your palms begin to sweat? Most likely, you quickly check the speedometer.

How long does it take for your heart to begin to slow down after the police car passes you?

Are you someone who feels ill at the sight of blood?

What about that strange sensation of discomfort in the waiting room of your doctor or your dentist?

And what happens when you smell fresh baked bread?

And what does *any* of this have to do with the treatment of habit disorders?

Quite a bit actually, but more of that later.

SOME THEORY

In their early works, *Patterns of the Hypnotic Techniques of Milton H. Erickson* (1975) and *Structure of Magic* (1975), Richard Bandler and John Grinder used the term "anchor" to describe the common neurological occurrence of paired associations, which they describe as "see-feel," "hear-feel," and "smell-feel" (surely taste-feel and touch-feel also occur). In general, the second (or "feel") part of the association is an inner feeling state, such as joy, anxiety, calm, fear, etc., while the first is generally externally generated sensory input. They note that the neurologists have described neural crossovers between different sensory modalities and psychologists are well aware of these concepts as exemplified clearly in the stimulus-response model of the behaviorist school of thought. Those therapists familiar with desensitization (reciprocal inhibition) therapy will be quite comfortable with this concept.

What seems to be unique about Bandler and Grinder's description is best demonstrated in this paragraph from *Neuro-Linguistic Programming*, Volume I:

> Anchoring is in many ways simply the user-oriented version of the "stimulus response" concept in behavioristic models. There are, however, some major differences between the two. These include: 1) Anchors do not need to be conditioned over long periods of time in order to become established. That kind of conditioning undoubtedly *will* contribute to the establishment of the anchor, but it is often the initial experience that establishes the anchor most firmly. Anchors then promote the use of single trial learning. 2) The association between the anchor and the response need not be directly reinforced by any immediate outcome resulting from the association in order to be established. That is, anchors, or associations, will become established without direct rewards or reinforcement for the association. Reinforcement, like conditioning, *will* contribute to the establishment of an anchor, but it is not required. 3) Internal experience (i.e., cognitive behavior) is considered to be as significant, behaviorally, as the overt measurable responses, in other words NLP (Neuro-Linguistic Programming) asserts that an internal dialogue, picture or feeling constitutes as much of a response as the salivation of Pavlov's dog (Dilts, Grinder, Bandler, Bandler and DeLozier, 1980, p. 120).

The matter is actually less complicated than it seems. We are merely talking about why we feel good when we hear our friend's voice on the telephone – even if she hasn't said much more than "hello." It is the everyday phenomenon of learning to associate certain internal states with specific external stimuli. What is so clinically important about anchoring is the notion of one-trial learning.

It is important to point out that the connection is not conscious, but rather automatic or unconscious. There appears to be no intermediate step to consciousness, such as, "Oh, I hear the siren and that makes me worry." The sound of the siren elicits tachycardia (rapid heart rate) and sweating palms directly. It is obvious that anchors are neither good nor bad. They most likely exist as a way to increase the efficiency of our information processing, allowing rapid decision-making. Sometimes, however, the effect is dysfunctional, triggering undesired behaviors. This is particularly true in habit disorders, as well as in phobias.

ANCHORS AND HABIT DISORDERS

"I always have a cigarette when I'm talking on the phone."

"I look at my watch, see it's 6 p.m., and I'm hungry for dinner, even though I had a late lunch."

"If I'm driving down the road and see a liquor or cocktail sign – that's it – I don't have a chance!"

It's important in the initial interview to learn what is anchored to your particular patient's problem, asking specifically, "When do you usually overeat? Where are you? What are you doing?" If the patient is vague, ask him or her to spend the next week gathering precise data about when he or she eats inappropriately. The therapist must be sure to make this request quite clear, inasmuch as specific information is required. The problem may be too much food or food at the wrong time or perhaps the wrong kinds of food. In giving the patient such an assignment, the therapist emphasizes that the patient should in no way alter the usual pattern of the habit. Interestingly though, this frequently occurs. Simply focusing the patient's awareness on the habitual behavior may be helpful in promoting change. Likewise, instructing the patient *not* to change may lead to change (see section on Directives in Chapter 5). If no change occurs, then the patient is just following your directives, of course, and there is "no problem." Should the patient return with "unexpected" positive results, it would be *unwise* to consider this the sole intervention or to explain to the patient why she has changed her behavior by making a comment such as the following: "See, I told you to eat so you stopped; you really are stubborn and oppositional." Rather, one could safely comment, "Gee, that's strange. I don't understand it since we haven't begun to do any of our interventions yet," and leave the issue there. The goal for *this* particular assignment is learning the patient's vulnerable situations so that these can be addressed specifically in the course of hypnotherapy.

SOME COMMON ANCHORS

You'll discover, as you inquire, the particular associations or anchors for each individual person. Recall again that these anchors function out of awareness. With this in mind, it would be confusing and unprofitable, if not counter-therapeutic, to ask, "What makes you have a cigarette?" Rather, the therapist's goal is to determine from the patient the following: "Where are you and what are you doing when you find yourself reaching for a cigarette?" We have found the following to be common:

Eating

There are some people who indeed eat by the clock without any awareness of a sensation of hunger. "I found myself looking at the clock and noting that it was almost twelve o'clock and I found that I became ravenous." We believe it is unproductive to wonder whether or not the person actually had the sensation of hunger when she went to eat for surely she believed that she did. As we said in Chapter 1, you are what you believe. If you believe you are hungry, you're hungry.

"Whenever I'm at home at night, I'm okay unless I pass the kitchen and see the refrigerator and then I can't stop myself from getting something to eat."

"When the kids start screaming, I'll eat anything in sight."

"When I'm watching TV and a commercial comes on, I immediately run to the kitchen."

Smoking

"My car can't possibly start without a cigarette in my mouth."

Another frequent belief of smokers is that you can't possibly talk on the phone without a cigarette in your mouth.

Maybe the most common behavioral anchor associated with smoking is eating. Smokers will inevitably smoke during or after meals or snacks.

"As soon as I sit down to talk with some friends, I light up."

Another common anchor for smoking is drinking alcoholic beverages. This is a special problem for therapists who have patients who want to stop smoking, but who drink more than occasionally and have no interest in changing their drinking behavior. Besides the association between alcohol and cigarettes, alcohol has a disinhibitory effect and breaks down the conscious willpower of the patient. We suggest that therapists may want to not take on such patients under a contract to quit smoking only.

Drinking

"When I'm getting together with people, the first thing I do is have a drink."

"When I go out the door at the end of the day, I head straight for the bar."

As is true for all habit disorders, drinking is often associated with stress. Whenever the problem drinker gets his cues that his particular stress is about to begin, such as the start of a fight in an unhappy marriage, he will reach immediately for the bottle or glass.

THE ANCHORING PARADIGM

Now that you've begun to recognize the powers of anchors and have started to identify them for your patient, we would like to explain how this information can be useful in treating habit disorders.

The concept of anchors enables us to understand the automatic and powerful unhealthy responses that habit disordered patients can display. The concept of anchors has also led to the development by Bandler and Grinder (1979) of a clinical technique called *anchoring*, which utilizes this particular conceptual understanding. It is a highly effective (usually one-shot) technique that associates a positive feeling, such as the feeling of being powerful, the feeling of being in control or the feeling of relaxation, with a new desired pattern of behavior in response to a cue that used to elicit the unhealthy pattern. This is done through the use of internal representations.

Below is a detailed case description of anchoring with a patient who came for help in controlling her eating and weight.

Laurel, 29, was being seen for overeating. She was aware of proper diet guidelines, but described some impediments to following these. She said that a particularly vulnerable time for her was in the company cafeteria at lunch break, when she found herself tempted by desserts. The following procedure, which demonstrates the use of anchoring for habit disorders, was performed.

The therapist told Laurel that, in order to perform

Verbalization

this particular intervention that would help her problem, it would be necessary for him to touch her on the shoulder, and asked if that would be okay with her. Receiving a yes answer, and utilizing Laurel's previous trance training, he asked her to go in her mind to a favorite place, telling her that this ideally would be a place in which she was comfortable and safe. Time was taken to deepen this trance experience by having her see, hear, and feel as much as possible all the sensations she usually experienced at this place. The therapist then continued:

"neutral" scene

"And now Laurel, I'd like you to let your mind drift away from this place for just a few moments, keeping this experience close by because we'll be going back to it. What I'd like you to do now is to remember a time in the past when you were really in control of a situation. (*The following is said forcefully in order to congruently communicate what is being suggested.*) Remember a time when you knew exactly what to do in a given situation. A time when you had every confidence that you knew just what to do and just what to say, and that the situation would turn out absolutely the way you wanted it to. And, indeed, you found this to be the case. And I'd like you to remember that, and when you've found such a situation, please let me know by nodding your head."

At this point, Laurel was given an opportunity to search through the catalogue of her memories for such an experience. When Laurel indicated that she was thinking about such a time, she was asked to intensify the experience as follows:

"Laurel, I'd like you now to imagine that you are having that experience again and to make it more intense by paying attention to all the things that you were seeing at that particular time, all the words and

Good for Calvet Stein

sounds that you heard, and the way you were talking to yourself and perhaps to others, and all the
good, strong, feelings you had. Please use all of your
sensory channels to intensify that experience now."

At this time, the therapist observed shifts in posture, changes in skin color with increased blood flow
to the lips and face, and a change in breathing from
shallow chest breathing to deeper abdominal breathing: the usual picture of a powerful person. When the
clinician saw these changes in physical appearance,
he grasped Laurel firmly on the shoulder and said,
"That's right, very good."

The therapist then removed his hand and asked
Laurel to drift back in her imagination to that favorite place. After she settled into that place for a while,
she was asked to imagine the next time in the future
that she would be in the cafeteria exposed to food
that she wants to eat but that she knows is not good
for her. She was instructed to give a signal when she
was doing so. When that occurred, the therapist then
said, "As you see the food there, say to yourself, 'No,
I don't need that.'" At precisely that moment, the
therapist touched her on the shoulder in exactly the
same way, "firing" the previously established control
anchor.

This procedure may occur several times, always focusing on a time in the future when in the past the
patient would have been in the vulnerable situation.
This part of the procedure (which is the actual therapy itself) established a relationship between the experience of saying "no" to the food, or any other behavior you want to encourage, and the feelings which
have been associated with the anchor, in this case,
power.

In the above example, the anchor is established by applying
any stimulus (in this case, grasping the shoulder) in conjunction

with the physical experience of the feelings of being in control
(or power or relaxation) which is elicited by requesting that the
individual imagine that the experiences are taking place. (This
is contrasted to having the patient *see oneself* having the experience. The latter dissociates the patient from the powerful
feeling and may not be as effective.) When establishing the anchor, you need to pay close attention to exactly where you are
touching the patient so that you can later touch the person in
the same place when the anchor is fired for the therapeutic intervention. In this instance, using a power anchor, the grasp
should be firm, so that it is congruent with the message of power
or being in control. It is usually maintained with the same intensity for 10 or 15 seconds.

The process of anchoring creates for the patient a relationship between an internal representation of a particular event
and a certain feeling. The clinician decides what feeling is appropriate. We have found the feeling of being in control or of
power to be most helpful with habit disorder cases. The clinician guides the patient in forming an internal representation of

an experience from the past which has been associated with such feelings. When the patient is experiencing what the therapist requested, he is asked to give a conscious indication that he has found such an episode. The clinician then asks the patient to intensify this experience by using all the sensory channels, visual, auditory and kinesthetic. At this point the clinician watches for behavioral changes associated with the desired feeling state.

We never move on from one step to the next without two indications that the patient is in an appropriate internal state. The first is the phenomenological self-description of a signal from the patient to the therapist. The second is the behavioral changes already described—changes in posture, skin color, and breathing.

When we are satisfied that the appropriate internal representation is occurring, we present the stimulus that is being used to establish the anchor. Therefore, the grasp on the shoulder in the above example becomes connected with the feeling state that the patient is experiencing at that time.

Let us stress once again that, in order to reproduce the feeling state, the stimulus (anchor) must be given in exactly the same way; for example, the touch on the shoulder must be given in the same place and with the same force. Obviously the stimulus which becomes anchored to the feeling state can be in any of the sensory modalities—visual, auditory, kinesthetic, olfactory or gustatory. For example, when there are indications that touching a patient may be inappropriate, we have commonly used the tapping of a pencil on a desk as an auditory stimulus. It is our preference, however, to use kinesthetic anchors in the treatment of habit disorders, because power can be easily conveyed analogically through the anchor itself, that is, by a firm touch. After the anchor has been established, it can then be used to provide the feeling state associated with it when appropriate, simply by reintroducing the stimulus.

As depicted in Laurel's case, the feeling state is used to provide a sense of power to be able to say "no" to food that is tempting the individual. In the last part of the procedure, the individual is asked to imagine in extensive detail events in the future that in the past had been difficult for him or her. The language that is used at this time is exceedingly important. This language itself literally puts the problem in the past tense. It becomes a problem the patient *used to have*, an elegant hypnotic suggestion.

A problem that occasionally occurs in treatment is that a patient has difficulty remembering a time when he or she was powerful, confident, or in control. When this happens, it may be necessary to explain to the patient that you know there have been many times in the past when that has occurred and you are simply asking for one of those times. Some individuals, usually those with depressive features, continue to draw a blank. From our experience, these people have had times in their lives when they have been powerful and masterful but they characteristically ignore them. Generally, they do not remember these experiences as distinct because they pay greater attention to the overall negative flow of feelings about their lives. Consequently, to help such persons regain a distinct, positive and powerful experience, you need to have them focus only on the experience itself. Often it is necessary to control the patient's communication and not allow the patient to disconfirm the positive experience with a "yes, but" statement, such as, "Yes, I really was in control, *but* then my boss came in and told me that I had made an error in some other area." At times, a helpful technique when a patient cannot access a positive, powerful experience is to allow the patient to identify with another person (see Chapter 5).

In working with habit disorders, this anchoring paradigm can be useful early in the treatment; it is also usually included in the technique of reframing (Chapter 6). It is not necessary to reestablish the anchor after the first session. Once an anchor is established it will function each time it is fired. Although this may seem very curious to some readers, it is consistent with our experience. In fact, when patients come in for follow-up sessions six months after an anchor has been established, they still respond appropriately when the stimulus is reintroduced.

OTHER CLINICAL USES OF ANCHORING

The paradigm of anchoring can be helpful to patients with habit disorders in a number of ways. For example, these patients often have been powerless not only in relation to cigarettes, food or alcohol, but in relationships with people. Consequently, an important part of treatment sometimes involves the patient's working on being more assertive with significant others. For example, an alcoholic patient became aware that coming home drunk was a way of asserting himself and "doing his own thing" in relationship to his wife. Otherwise, his stance in the marriage was generally passive and powerless. The patient decided that he wanted to say "no" to his wife and assert himself directly at times. After a power anchor was established, it was fired not only as he imagined himself saying "no" to alcohol but also as he envisioned himself acting assertively with his wife.

A conceptual understanding of the phenomenon of anchoring is important for all therapists; however, it can be especially important in the work of the clinical hypnotist. For example, most patients become naturally anchored to a "trance" chair and after a few inductions in that chair will spontaneously go into trance when sitting in it or sometimes even seeing it. The same principle applies to the hypnotist's voice. Patients become anchored to the sound of the voice and soon will spontaneously begin to develop trance anytime they hear it. This is useful not only for rapid inductions in your office but also in emergency situations when instructions can be given to the patient via the telephone.

Anchoring provides many creative opportunities for the clinical hypnotist. And you may wonder just how and when in the near future it will come in handy for you.

CHAPTER 4

INDIRECT COMMUNICATION

RECENTLY THE THREE of us were going to another state to conduct a workshop. This was a place that could not be entirely traveled to by plane, so after going as far as we could by air, we rented a car and began driving to our destination. Soon we realized we were lost, so we stopped at a gas station and asked the attendant how we could get to the other state. He said to us, "You make two lefts and three rights," and we thanked him and left. A few minutes down the road we realized that he didn't tell us in what order, so we decided to experiment. First we made a right, a left, a right and a left, and a right. But when we got there we realized that wasn't right so we had to go back from where we left, which required us to make a left, a right, a left, a right and a left. And then we were right back where we left from. This time we decided we would attempt to make two rights, a left, a right and a left. That wasn't right either. So to go back, we needed to make a right, a left, a right and two lefts, and once again we were right back where we started from.

We thought to ourselves, "How can we get to this other state?" This time we thought we would try a left, a left, a right, a right and a right. But as you can guess, that wasn't right either, and obviously to get right back to where we started, we had to make a left, a left, a left, a right and a right, and then we were

right back from where we left. We didn't know exactly what to do. We became a little anxious, but we thought there were other alternatives, and this time we tried a right, a left, a right, a right, a left, but frustratingly enough, that wasn't right either. Once again, to go back from where we began we had to make a right, two lefts, a right and a left and we were right back from where we started.

We became a little anxious, wondering if we would ever get to the other state. We thought this time we would make a right, a left, a left, a right and a right; but when we got to our destination, we found that wasn't right either, and we had to go back from where we left which required us to make a left, a left, a right, a right and a left. And we thought, "How could we ever get to this other state?"

Finally, we thought to ourselves that the right thing to do would be to take one deep breath and just let go; and then we'd find the right way to get to the other state, and once we were there, we knew how easy and enjoyable the learning we were about to partake in would be.

Whenever we communicate with another person, we are directing the information to both the right brain and left brain, or if you will, the unconscious and conscious mind. An effective hypnotic communicator will realize and take advantage of this. What we refer to as "indirect communication" is communication directed by the therapist to the patient's unconscious or right brain. This is indirect in that the intention of the communication is not fully consciously understood by the patient. As discussed in the previous chapter, contrary to many of the myths about Ericksonian hypnosis, not all therapeutic communication is meant to be indirect. However, these indirect communications can be of some of the most effective and even magical in the therapeutic process.

One of the major advantages of indirect communication is that it bypasses any conscious resistance a patient may have. As discussed in Chapter 1, communication that goes to the right brain is not influenced by all the language or ideas the left brain holds. You will remember the example of the person who drew the pink banana without understanding exactly why he drew a banana. Now imagine if the patient had come into the office with some notions that he or she did not like bananas, or could not draw bananas, and how those notions would interfere with drawing the banana. By bypassing the part of him or her that has these dysfunctional ideas (the conscious mind), the experimenter might influence the subject to draw a banana. We believe that all patients with some problems with habit control do have some dysfunctional ideas about what they can and cannot do in the left side of their brain or the conscious mind. Rather than talking logically to that side of the mind, as many "helpers" have done without success, we prefer to use the flexibility of another approach, tapping into resources in the unconscious mind that may be more helpful to the person in controlling a dysfunctional habit.

There are other important reasons why indirect communication is often effective in therapy. Sometimes we need to give patients a message that may be somewhat derogatory. When we do this, we know that patients (like all human beings) will have a psychological need to defend their ego integrity. The indirect communication techniques that will be presented in this chapter allow patients to listen to the material presented without feeling the need to reply defensively. Another advantage of these indirect techniques is that they allow patients to believe that the changes that are occurring are being made strictly by them. In other words, indirection reduces the apparent influence of the therapist. Even though these techniques may, in fact, be very controlling and direct, the patient will believe that these changes happen spontaneously or only as he directs, since the therapist will appear to be talking about someone or something else. This is one effective way of dealing with the complex problem of the therapist's being in control of the therapeutic situation and yet pursuing the eventual goal of the patient's taking more control over his or her life. Existentially speaking, what one believes to be true becomes true, so as patients begin to believe that they are making healthy changes by themselves, they often continue to make healthy changes and maintain a healthy life-style in a self-directed way.

The last major advantage of these approaches is that they are very creative and interesting for the health professional to use. In our profession, we struggle constantly with the two b's: *boredom* and *burnout*. There are only so many overweight people you can treat, smokers you can help, alcoholics you can influence, before this burnout occurs. By treating each patient as a unique personality, rather than as a symptom, and by using these creative techniques (especially storytelling), the professional can maintain a high level of interest in each and every case.

Indirect communication is an umbrella for a variety of specific techniques, limited only by our own imagination. In an earlier text (King et al., 1983), we listed many of these techniques with examples showing their use with different types of psychological and medical disorders. The examples below show how these techniques can be used for both trance induction and treatment of habit disorders. Let us emphasize that this is a small sample and the list of possibilities is endless.

EMBEDDED MESSAGES

Embedded commands or messages (sometimes called brack- eting or the interspersal technique) are small segments of larger statements that are signaled out for the attention of the un- conscious through the use of such behaviors as tonal shifts, pauses, or shifts in one's body. For example, if you would like to give someone the metaphoric message to learn to stand on his or her own two feet, you can begin by talking in some detail about how he learned to walk. You will talk about how he stood up, pulled himself up against a chair or sofa, took a step, fell down, stood up again; then you will say, "And pretty soon you learned to . . . " at which time you'll pause, raise your voice slight- ly, and say, "Stand on your own two feet, Fred," pause again, lower your voice again and continue on with your sentence. Through the use of tonal shifts and pauses, this message, "Stand on your own two feet, Fred," which in context is a logical part of a left brain message about learning to walk, will also stand out as a separate message to the right brain or unconscious.

An example of using an embedded suggestion to help a pa- tient "let go" (an important message during a trance induction) is the following:

> You know, I have a new book out with a picture
> of a roller coaster on the front cover, and when I am
> traveling around the country doing workshops, peo-
> ple often ask me, "Why do you have a picture of a
> roller coaster on the front of a professional book? I
> tell them it's for two reasons. First I just happen to
> love roller coasters – it's a hobby of mine. But second-
> ly, learning about how to ride a roller coaster is very
> much like learning about hypnosis – the secret is know-
> ing when to hold on, and knowing when to (*subtly
> raise your voice here and every other time you talk*

about letting go), let go, Fred. For example, my daughter is only 11, and yet she is already a roller coaster
freak just like her dad. She knows the secret to riding
a roller coaster is knowing that there are times it's
safe and comfortable for her to hold on tight, such as
when the roller coaster is going down the hill and
around the fast bend. But, do you know, Fred, we've
observed that there are many people who never let
go when they are riding a roller coaster. And when
the ride is over they end up with sore hands, tight
elbows, strains in the back, pains in the neck or even
headaches. Now my daughter already knows that
there are many times that the way to enjoy a roller
coaster is to, *let go, Fred.* For example, when the
roller coaster is going up a hill and you can literally
hear the clanking of the chains, that is a good time
to sit back, enjoy the view and, *let go, Fred.* Or when
the roller coaster is near the top of the hill, and you
could enjoy the view of the park; that's another time
to, *let go, Fred*, knowing that both your intuition or
unconscious mind, as we call it, and your conscious
mind will let you know when it is safe and necessary
to hold on again.

By telling this story in a relaxed way during the trance induction, the hypnotist can offer Fred the embedded message to "let
go" a number of times without appearing to just be ordering him
to let go — something which very few people are able to do under
orders.

Here is another example of an embedded message that may
be used in conjunction with weight control. While talking about
another patient casually, mentioning how we might be helping
him or her use hypnosis for pain control, we begin to talk about
how we teach people to alter sensations in their body by using
an arm levitation. During that conversation, we would talk
about how after coming to the office the patient would learn to,
get lighter, and lighter, each week. Again, the command to get
lighter and lighter each week would be set off through the use

useful tip for estimating duration of therapy (esp. in obesity)

of pauses, tonal shifts, or maybe by having the hypnotist lean forward and be closer to the patient, as those specific words and only those specific words are mentioned.

TALKING TO OR ABOUT SOMEONE ELSE

Another effective means of indirect communication is to talk either to another professional within earshot of the patient or to the patient directly about someone else, such as another patient. This technique is particularly effective in gathering information during the initial intake sessions or in getting messages across that may require a defensive reply. For example, in order to pace a belief system about how long it may take a patient to lose the desired weight, you can begin talking about other patients who have come to see you for similar problems. You can say how Patient A came and, quicker than you thought possible, say in about a month's time, was able to lose the 30 pounds. You could then mention Patient B, who took two or three months to complete his work. You then could discuss Patient C who did exactly what she needed to do, but took about six months to reach her desired weight. All the while, you can watch the nonverbal responses of the patient, and if you are a good observer you can usually discern what she believes is likely to occur. After gathering this information you can turn to the patient and say, "And after looking over your case records, I believe it will probably take you three or four months to do what you need to do for yourself." In this way, you can give the patient an optimistic statement that hopefully will become a self-fulfilling prophecy about the successful treatment, and do it in a manner that she is likely to accept because it is in pace with her belief system.

Consider another example: You have directed an alcoholic patient to go to AA meetings. However, based on his or her past record, you believe it is likely that the patient probably has not fulfilled the required directives for that week. Instead of directly confronting the patient again (which sometimes, of course, would be the desired treatment), you may choose to bypass the rationalizations and arguments that are likely to occur. This can

be accomplished by casually mentioning to your nurse or secretary, within earshot of this patient, Mrs. Jones who came in yesterday and did not do whatever she was directed to do, and how you threw her out of treatment and told her that you just couldn't help her and wouldn't see her again until she fulfilled your directives for at least three weeks in a row. This is an effective way to give a patient a warning about the consequences of not following the directives without arousing his defenses.

An interesting variation of this theme involves using the telephone. The therapist can arrange for the patient to overhear a conversation with another "patient" or "professional." We often use the weather lady as an effective co-worker. We dial the weather recording just before the patient enters the office and then pretend to be talking to another patient or professional about another patient. This is a very effective way of clearly getting a message across to a patient without requiring him to "dig in" and defend his current behavior.

ILLUSION OF CHOICE

This simple but highly effective technique involves occupying the patient's conscious mind with choices that seem to give him a lot of freedom of choice, although the bottom line of any choice offered is a contract with the therapist to do something that he directs for the patient's best interest. There are many examples of this technique that can be used in both the induction process and in treating habit disorders.

First, here are three brief examples of using illusions of choice as part of the trance induction. Since, as we mentioned in Chapter 1, we believe that the depth of trance is irrelevant to the treatment outcome, we may ask patients at the beginning of a session, "Would you like to go into a light, medium or deep trance today?" The person's mind consciously begins to think about what he believes to be the difference between light, medium and deep, and then makes a choice, oftentimes without consciously realizing that what he is contracting to do is the second half of the statement, that is, go into a trance. When a patient says to us that today he will go into a medium trance, we not only do not care, but in fact, do not even really know what he means by a medium trance. His notion of a medium trance may be significantly different from our notion. The key is that he has agreed to go into a trance and is likely to fulfill that psychological contract.

Likewise, we often ask a patient when she enters the room, "Would you like to sit in this chair and go into a trance today, or would you like to sit in that chair and go into a trance today?" Her conscious mind becomes occupied with the chairs, which seems more comfortable, etc., without consciously realizing that when she says "this chair," she has agreed to the second half of the contract, "and go into a trance today."

At the end of a trance, we like to suggest to patients that sometime within the next minute or two of clock time, whenever they are ready, they will begin to feel more alert, open their eyes and reorient themselves to the room. Again, there is an illusion of choice, a suggestion that they could do it anytime they want, but in reality the limits have been set — "in the next minute or two." This gives the appearance of a very permissive type of treatment, which patients appreciate, and yet the therapist gets what is desired, in that the patient quickly comes out of trance and does not sit there for 15 or 20 minutes, taking up office time and space.

In treatment, there are many times when you may want to use illusions of choice. For example, with a new weight patient, we may ask, "Would you like to start your diet this week, or would you like to start next week after the second session?" Again, the bottom line is that she is going to start her diet. While the technique gives the appearance that there are many choices in the treatment process, in fact the choices are quite limited.

One of our favorite illusions of choice for treatment involves using days of the week. We may give a patient a directive (see Chapter 5), and then suggest that he or she can do it anytime in the next week, whenever he or she chooses. Then we might go on:

I think you'll do it on Friday. Even though any day would be *OK*, most of my patients who like me seem to do things on Friday, which is the day I usually do my own personal growth work. Now, maybe you'll do it on a Monday or a Tuesday, but I think you'll probably do it on a Friday. Some patients do it in the middle of the week, like Wednesday or Thursday, but I think you'll do it on a Friday. It's even possible you'll do it over the weekend, but I think it'll be Friday.

The patient has two choices. He can see himself has a person cooperating with us and doing exactly what we want, and therefore do it on Friday. Or he can hold onto that little part of himself that would like to resist us, to prove that he is not under our control, and therefore he may do it any day of the week other than Friday. Of course, the effect is that he will follow our directive; we really do not care what day he does it.

THERAPEUTIC DOUBLE BINDS

A therapeutic double bind occurs when the therapist puts the patient in a situation where, no matter what he does, the outcome is both predictable and therapeutic. It differs from the above-mentioned illusion of choice in that the patient is not as consciously aware of the different options that are available. Examples of therapeutic double binds are seen in many of the elementary trance inductions which most readers probably already know. One example is as follows:

Induction verbalization

Now, I'd like you to imagine a chalkboard in your mind. It could be any color – black, green, gray, light blue; it could be one you've seen before or one you just make up for this occasion; it doesn't matter. When you see this chalkboard in your head, I'd like you to let me know by nodding your head. (*Assuming here the patient nods and can do internal visualization.*) Now, I'd like you not to begin until I finish the directions. What I'd like you to do, when I tell you to begin, is walk up to the chalkboard, and in your imagination, write down the number 100. When you can see the number, and only when you could see it, I'd like you to say it out loud so I could hear it. When you say the number out loud, the number will erase itself or disappear in some way, and then I'd like you to write the next lower number, that is, 99. Again, when you see the number, say it, when you say it, it will erase itself or disappear, and then I'd like you to write the next lower number. Now, the numbers will get more and more difficult for you to see and say, but I'd like you to try to get to zero. And when you get to zero, or when you can't see or say them anymore, whichever happens first, I'd like you to erase the chalkboard from your mind and take yourself in your imagination to some place you'd like to be.

These instructions constitute a therapeutic double bind because they are given in such a manner that the patient will do one of two things. Either she will do what you have told her and try hard (and succeed) to get to zero; of course, almost anyone is likely to go into trance after concentrating that long on an internal visualization. If she does this, she will feel that she has followed your directions by getting to zero, is cooperative and in a trance or at least beginning the process of trance induction. Of course, if the numbers get too hard to see and say and she cannot get to zero, she has also cooperated, since this is something you suggested would happen. That becomes proof that she is, in fact, a "good trance subject." Whatever she does, she is likely to be binded into going into a trance and to believing that she is a cooperative subject.

A therapeutic double bind can also be useful in the case of a patient who has trouble saying "no" to people he or she sees as authority figures, including a spouse. During reframing, you and the patient may come to realize that one of the secondary gains the patient gets from smoking is that this is the only way he or she can say no to a spouse who is clearly on his back about smoking. A therapeutic double bind would be to give the patient a directive that during the next week he is to go home and say "no" very clearly at least two or three times to his boss or spouse. The double bind is that the patient will either have to go home and say "no" or in effect say "no" to you, another authority figure, by not doing what you direct him to do. Either way, the patient will be binded into saying "no" to an authority figure, which at times can be a therapeutic change in behavior.

CONTINGENCY SUGGESTIONS

Using contingency suggestions involves linking a suggestion with some preceding undeniable fact or facts, even though there is no necessary logical reason for the connection. Contingency suggestions (sometimes called "junko logic") are a form of pacing and leading.

> You know what it's like to go outside on a cold, wintry day and feel the wind cut across the uncovered part of your skin. You know what it's like to go outside on a warm, spring day and feel the sun permeate your body. You know what it's like to listen to music that surprises you because it's unexpectedly powerful and pleasant. You know what it's like to see and hear the sound of rain drops on the window of your car or house, and because you have all these sensory experiences inside of you, you have the ability to do all the work that is necessary to do for yourself during this next week.

We commonly include this passage in conversational inductions while we are doing trance work with patients. It is a suggestion that the patient has the ability to do all that he needs to do for himself, and the proof of the suggestion is that he has had all these sensory experiences. Now the sensory experiences are inevitable; every patient who comes into our office will have had these experiences. However, the relationship between these experiences and his ability to do some therapeutic work during the next week is quite dubious. When these connections are made in a quite natural and easy manner, the patient will often accept the suggestion without question.

We sometimes hook up the suggestion for therapeutic change

with current or ongoing events. For example, we might say, "Since it's a beautiful day today, this therapy session will be a significant one for you," or, "Because the Baltimore Orioles are on a winning streak, you'll be noticing increased control over your behavior."

By the way, since you're reading this book right now, you may begin to get curious about exactly how soon you will be able to effectively use these techniques in your own practice.

CONFUSION

Just like Arizona in August, confusion is a very uncomfortable state to be in, and most people will do anything reasonable to get out of it. We often say confusing things during trance work to help patients obtain certain goals. An example of a confusion technique, of course, is the beginning of this chapter. Imagine that conversation three or four times as long as it is presented in this book — and see if you know what state you are in then!

We find that when patients are confused they are likely to do one of three things. The first is to go into a trance in order to avoid the confusion. When we work together, sometimes two or all three of us will simultaneously tell different stories, all of which have many left-right connotations. When we debrief patients we find that often they alter their sensory perception (a clear trance behavior) in order to deal with the ensuing confusion. What they tell us is that they heard one of us and not the other one or two, or sometimes they did not hear any of us at all.

Another possible way of dealing with confusion is to fill in blanks or add words that seem to let a statement make sense. Oftentimes, at the beginning of a trance induction and after referring to the unconscious, we will make a statement such as, "and many people ask us exactly what is the unconscious, but you know, and we know, and that's all right." On the surface, that is a very nonsensical statement, but you would be surprised how many people feel, after the trance, that we have discussed the nature of the unconscious and are in perfect agreement as to exactly what it is.

The third possibility is that many people will take the first logical, helpful suggestion to lead them out of confusion. We often confuse a subject and then follow the confusion with a direct therapeutic suggestion, which the patient is apt to accept.

If you want to learn more about the interesting effects of confusion, we would suggest that you do this. The next time your telephone rings, pick up the phone and say, "Hello, is John there?" It is very likely that there will be a noticeable pause on the other end as that person experiences trance behavior.

The great philosopher Friedrich Nietzsche was discussing the discomfort of an unknowing state like confusion, as well as how we make up our own realities (see Chapter 1), when he said:

> With the unknown, one is confronted with danger, discomfort, and care; the first instinct is to abolish these painful states. First principal: any explanation is better than none. Since at the bottom it is merely a matter of wishing to be rid of oppressive representations, one is not too particular about the means of getting rid of them: the first representation that explains the unknown as familiar feels so good that one considers it true. The proof of pleasure as a criteria of truth (1968).

METAPHORIC COMMUNICATION

Human beings have learned to understand their place in the world and communicate with each other by effectively using symbols and metaphors. Generally speaking, a metaphor may be described as a communication in which one thing is described or expressed in terms of another. As a result, some new light is shed or some new learning takes place in reference to that which is being described. Unfortunately, much of our training, in its attempt to imitate scientific rigor, has negated the important aspect of metaphoric communication.

If a friend came to you and said she had a heavy heart, you would not look for a scale to weigh it. Instead, you would intuitively know what that meant, and would be able to suggest that maybe there were things she could do to lighten the load. Unfortunately, many medical and social scientists have learned that what they need to do with a patient who has a "heavy heart" is to get her to describe in much more detail exactly what she is feeling, all the events leading up to the "heaviness," etc., as if somehow the designation of a heavy heart in and of itself is not enough information.

We need to learn to pay attention to the metaphoric language of patients and to pace it back to them. For example, if your patient were a sports fan or amateur athlete, rather than talk to him in detail about his existential responsibility to make the changes necessary in life at times when he's stuck, you might look him right in the eye and say, "I've done what I can; the ball's in your court now."

Clinicians need to understand body language and symptoms themselves as the patient's metaphoric expression of what is happening in his life, and then use that understanding to effectively communicate with that patient. For example, if an overweight adolescent has overbearing parents, it might be helpful to pace him by saying, "You may have to swallow a lot from your parents." Or, "It must be hard to stomach all the things that have happened to you at home." In the same way, a youngster might come in with noticeable skin rashes. Instead of asking the patient about the rash in an analytic or traditional medical way, you may want to just ask, "Who's getting under your skin this week?" You'll be surprised at the quick, uninhibited responses from patients when you understand their symptoms metaphorically and speak back to them in that same metaphoric language. Cigarette smokers (and patients with ulcers) will often comment about how a person or situation "burns me up" or "makes me fume." Such comments strongly hint that healthier patterns of behavior to deal with anger would be a productive focus of therapy.

In the next chapter, the use of directives will be discussed in some detail. Let us point out here, however, that with many patients directives may best be given metaphorically in order to avoid some of the initial defensiveness around the symptomatology. For example, if the patient seems stuck at a given life stage and just cannot seem to make the changes necessary to move toward health, you may want to give him the metaphorical directive to go home, choose one room of the house and totally change it. The directive should include instructions to take every single thing out of the room, other than wall-to-wall carpeting, and put the room back together again in a somewhat different way. Very few patients who are making an effort in therapy will have trouble with this directive, even though they may have significant problems changing something important about their lives. The surprising thing about this work is that after the patient has followed the metaphoric directive, direct change seems to come with surprising ease and to occur in such a way that the patient feels responsible for initiating the change, rather than seeing himself as following the therapist's directive.

Another variation of metaphoric communication involves directing the patient to have certain imagining take place during self-hypnosis or to experience certain dreams as he is first going to sleep, even while he retains some control over the content. For example, we often ask patients during self-hypnosis to use their imagination to go upstairs to the basement of their mind or downstairs to their attic (confusion technique) and to locate some excess baggage that has been stored there. We ask them to notice details about this baggage, such as exactly what color it might be, its shape, its size, etc. We might suggest some characteristics about the excess baggage that, in some way, match the patient's symptoms. For example, for an overweight patient we might say that the baggage takes up a lot of space and has been weighing the person down. We let patients know that in many people's basements or attics there is a lot of excess baggage, and that they may only want to get rid of one or two pieces right now. We tell them that sometimes people know exactly what is inside this extra luggage, but sometimes people only know that the luggage is there without knowing exactly about the content. For the first week we ask them to just make inventories of their home and find out something about this excess baggage. The next week, or sometimes even during trance work in our office, we direct them to take this excess baggage one piece at a time and to find some way to get rid of it. We make lots of alternative suggestions to help them. We tell them that some people in their imaginations go out to the back of their house where their trash cans are and place the baggage there and wait for the trashman to come. Other people go to the bathroom, open up the bags and flush the contents down the toilet. Some people take the baggage to the neighborhood grocery store, where there are always large trash bins, and dump it there immediately. We tell them we do not know exactly what they are going to do, but that in some way, in our office or at night when they are doing self-hypnosis or in their dreams, during that week they can find ways to get rid of this excess luggage or baggage. Again, the productive work that people report that incidentally happens to them during the ensuing weeks is amazing. They do not usually even make a conscious connection between the metaphoric imaging that they are experiencing in trance or dream work and their behavioral changes during the rest of the week.

THE ART OF STORYTELLING

One morning while writing the first draft of this book, the three of us flipped on the TV to try to get some sport scores from the previous night. We came across a Sunday morning preacher. We could tell by the man's body language and the tone of his voice that he was just about to start an interesting story, so we left the TV on for a few moments. He told the story about a much heralded football game in Birmingham, Alabama. He said that even though it was heralded, it actually wasn't much of a game because one side was much bigger and stronger than the other side. He went on to describe the game in some interesting detail and noted that towards the end of the game the underdog team was losing — but only by less than a touchdown. As time was running out, the underdog's coach called a timeout and said to his team, "Look boys, we can win this game. Even though they're bigger than us, Albert's faster than any of them; he can outrun them. Give the ball to Albert and we can win this game." The team went back on the field. The first play Albert didn't get the ball and nothing much happened. The coach was bewildered. The second play the team didn't give the ball to Albert and nothing much good happened, and again the coach was bewildered, as well as angry. The same thing happened on the third and fourth plays, and the team lost the game. When it was over, the coach said to the quarterback, "Why didn't you give the ball to Albert?" The quarterback answered, "Albert didn't want the ball!" The preacher went on to explain the moral by discussing Albert's reluctance to take a risk and by using such metaphors as, "You don't swing at anything—you don't hit anything," and, "You can't steal second with one foot tied to first."

We thought of all the times we have heard counselors and therapists trying to explain to patients how living in an over-protected way gives the illusion of safety but guarantees defeat in the long run. We have never seen any therapists get the message across to the patient as well as this preacher got it across to his audience on this particular Sunday morning.

Since the beginning of recorded history, storytelling, in both oral and written form, has helped mankind pass down culture, "socialize the young," and help solve problems. Almost all religions are maintained and based on the art of storytelling. Storytelling has some natural properties that allow it to fit in very nicely with our understanding of hypnotic work. First of all, a well told story is, in itself, naturally mesmerizing. A story told with animation, changing tones, and the correct body posture or gesture by the speaker encourages right brain imagery to literally depict the story, and this experience can be understood as a trance. An alternative to this is a boring story with a lot of details, which after a while encourages the person to go into a trance just to avoid the boredom. Milton Erickson claimed that if nothing else he could bore people into trances as he talked in his low, slow voice about all his family members.

A second important advantage of storytelling is that it allows the therapist to metaphorically implant strategies for change about a particular problem, and yet to do so in such an indirect way that the conscious resistance of the patient is not generated. The success of therapeutic storytelling depends on both one's ability to effectively use the process and the content of the story itself. Before describing how to make up the *content* of a story, let us offer three basic rules of how to *deliver* the story. The first rule is that it must be told casually, almost as an aside to the therapeutic or medical interaction. Remember, once a patient sits down to talk about his "problem," his defenses are on alert. However, before this therapeutic process starts, or after it is finished, or in the middle as you are taking a casual break and drifting off into chitchat, the patient's defenses are naturally down. At those times, the patient is open in the fullest sense, both consciously and unconsciously, to understanding what you have to say.

The second rule of telling a story is that there has to appear to be some logical reason for doing so. We often lead into a story by saying, "Boy, I'm glad I made it to the office today because something unusual just happened to me," or "You know, I've been thinking about you all week, because I just realized that I have an old friend I haven't seen for a long time who looks exactly like you, even though she's a few years younger." We then proceed to tell the story about the friend or about what happened to us that morning. Students often say to us that these stories are so transparent that the patient must clearly understand that there is some message directed at him. After all, professionals just do not tell off-the-cuff stories. Our experience is quite the opposite. If the story is told confidently, in a natural, casual way, and with some clear rationale, the patient will listen attentively to the story—just as we would like.

The third rule of storytelling, which we will discuss further at the end of this chapter, is that you never analyze or process the story; in fact, the second you finish it you go right on to another topic.

Stories are constructed in one of two ways. First are those stories that have implanted within them a strategy for change that you would like the patient to adopt. The second type of story has no strategy for change, possibly because you are not sure exactly what the patient needs to do; rather, it appeals to the person's right brain or unconscious, which is understood to be the creative part of each individual, to solve the problem for him. Below are examples of both to help clarify the differences between them.

First, let us look at stories developed for habit disorder patients that send a certain message or implant a certain strategy within the patient.

You know, I have a friend named Anne, who reminds me of you a lot, she looks a lot like you. She's a little bit taller and a couple of years younger. Anne and I grew up in Baltimore together and recently I was back there visiting and saw her after not seeing her for years, and she told me some interesting things. Like many women in our culture, Anne thought the only way she could be happy was to be with men, and she thought the only way she could be with men was to say "yes" every time one wanted to go to bed. She told me recently that even though she likes sex, she was beginning to feel more and more alienated from herself and her body because she felt like she didn't have enough control to say "no" to sex. Recently, when I saw Anne she told me a story about how she had been out with a man she liked, and as usual, at the end of the night he suggested that they go to bed. For some reason, on this occasion Anne said "no." I don't know what happened to Anne and that particular man, but the nice thing that happened to her, she said, was that for the very first time she felt in charge of herself and she no longer felt the victim of her habits or social pressures. Now, the change in her sexual behavior is really not all that important; but the great change that took place in Anne is how much better she began to feel about herself in all aspects of her life. And you know that how you feel about yourself is the most important thing in the world. It permeates your family life, your social life, your work life.

The above story can be used with anybody who needs to learn to say "no." There are two major advantages. First, by talking about sex rather than the topic of the patient's complaint (food, drugs, smoking, etc.), the message is given indirectly and the patient does not need to be defensive; after all, she is not there to talk about sex. Second, the story implants a reward; that is, if you do say "no" and take control and stop being the victim of your habits, you will get good feelings about yourself. These feelings are then described as really the most important in the world, in that they permeate every part of your life. Again, this story should be told casually with a seeming connection to the patient; also, after finishing the story the therapist should go right on to the next topic at hand.

The next story gets across the message about the "friendly enemy." In order to pace people's habits, the therapist has to let them know that the therapist understands that at one time the unhealthy habit was a friend. For many people, a pack of cigarettes was the only friend they had during many a lonely night. Food comforted them in moments of stress, or alcohol helped reduce unbearable tension. Pretending that these are nothing but "dirty, rotten" habits, without understanding their friendly aspects, does not pace the patients' experience. The following story paces both the nature of the one-time friendly habit and the patient's present need to give up that habit.

> You know, Frank, I was thinking this week about your family. You have a daughter who is going to be going to college in a year or two, and I was just reminiscing about what a stressful time that was in my life. In high school I had a friend named Mo. We were inseparable; people thought of us practically as Siamese twins. We did everything together, both at school and at play. We went to the University of Maryland together, and we were roommates in our freshman year, but just as we got to college, something started to happen. It soon became apparent that Mo and I were going in different directions. I wanted to do well in college and be a professional.

Mo wanted to use the opportunity to do nothing but party. Even though I like to party well enough and certainly did it occasionally, I soon discovered that if I did what Mo wanted me to do, and continued the close friendship, I was going to be flunking out of school within a semester or two. It was a hard choice but eventually the strain became so great, I had to give up Mo as a friend. It was difficult to do and a very sad moment for me, but I realized that even though he had been a great friend at one time, he was becoming an enemy, and that if I followed the lead of where his friendship was taking me, I would have never gotten to where I knew I wanted to get to in life. And even though it was a very tense time for me and created some problems in my own mind, I did what I had to do. Of course, looking back in my life, I have no regrets whatsoever. I hope your daughter doesn't have to go through some of the same stresses.

This story illustrates several points we have already mentioned. It was a pace for the person in that it recognized both the stress of doing the task at hand (giving up a habit) and the fact that the habit had at some time in his life played an important supportive role. It was indirect, because I was talking about my friend in college, partying and grades, and nothing about the patient's habit. The last statement about his daughter was actually just a distraction to add to the concrete reason for telling the story and to begin to move off the story onto something else.

The following stories are told to patients when the clinician is not exactly sure what the payoff involved is or exactly what the new needed strategy is, but trusts that inside the person's unconscious there is a solution. The purpose of these stories is to activate that part of the person that has the answer and allow it to begin to influence the person's behavior.

The first story was told to a nurse who had come in for treatment of a moderate alcohol problem. It was clear that one of the things maintaining the problem was constant nagging about her drinking from her parents and physician friends. The woman needed some way to resist her friends and family, whom she saw as "overbearing," but neither she nor the therapist could figure out consciously a good alternative. The following story is actually an example of indirect reframing, in that it helped the patient find new, more acceptable alternatives.

You know, Lillie, I have a lot of nurses as friends, and just this week I ran across one I hadn't seen for a year. Her name is Lisa. Lisa has her R.N and a B.S. degree in psychology, and has been enjoying her present job for a number of years, but over the past year has begun to get a little bored. Her parents and the head nurse are on her back something terrible, trying to get her to go to nursing school for a Master's degree. There is a part of Lisa that clearly wants to do this, but for some reason that she wasn't even sure about, there was something inside of her that just didn't want to go. She got confused and felt kind of trapped, and so one day when she had nothing to do, she went back to see her favorite old teacher from her R.N. program. She told everything about what was happening to this old teacher, and the teacher said, "Before you decide about going back to school or not, I suggest that you try something else out that I want to tell you." The old nurse then leaned down and told Lisa a secret. Lisa took three vacation days from work and just disappeared. It worried her family and friends a lot because no one knew where she was. When she did come back she seemed more cheerful and within a week had enrolled in the Master's program at the university's nursing school, It's a strange story to me — I don't even know what the secret was, but it was just a coincidence that I have you, a nurse, as a new patient and I happened to see my old nursing friend this very past week, and she had all these strange things happen to her. I guess it really doesn't mean anything. Anyway, let's get on with your work now.

Metaphor is an effective way to appeal to the unconscious or right brain part of a person. We always pick an old wise teacher, a master architect, an old grandparent, an old dusty textbook, etc., as representing the unconscious part of the person. We then tell some story where the character with whom the patient will identify gets some new information from this source and is able to use it in a helpful way. Obviously, since in these examples we do not have a strategy to implant, if the patient ever asks what the secret was, or what the book said, we just shrug our shoulders and say, "I don't know—I was never told."

Here is another story that can be generally useful in a variety of clinical situations. Once again, this story does not suggest specific strategies for change, but leaves that up to the patient's own unconscious resources.

You know, the other night I had an interesting dream. I woke up in a strange, but somewhat familiar bed in a strange room. I walked down several flights of stairs of the house until I got to the basement. When I looked around the basement I noticed that the beams that went from the floor to the ceiling were rather warped and in a state of disrepair. I saw electrical wiring hanging from the rafters and I could tell that there were some short circuits. I saw the plumbing and it really looked rusted and in need of other work too. As I walked out the basement door, some workers were coming down the stairs to the basement. There was an electrician carrying all kinds of wiring and switches and dials and levers and circuits and fuses. There was a carpenter and I noticed a tool box full of all kinds of tools. And I saw a plumber. I walked outside and up some steps to the ground. I walked around the side of the house, and when I got to the front I could see that there was some kind of carnival or fair going on. There were booths set up in the street and on some of the walks, and many people were milling around. I walked down the street and, now and then, some people walked by. I smiled but my perception was that I didn't get a smile back.

People were in their own little groups having a lot of fun. But I began to feel kind of lonely and alienated and confused. I felt very hurt. I turned around and went back up the street and walked around the side of the house again. As I went down the cellar steps, the workers were leaving. I went in the cellar and I saw all the wonderful work that they had done. The beams from the foundation to the ceiling had been shorn up. I could see that they were a lot stronger and more sturdy. I could see all kinds of new wiring and a new box of circuit breakers. And I saw some new electrical components, like switches and dials. I could see the shiny, new plumbing and could just imagine how easily things could flow. Suddenly, I felt quite good and I went back out the cellar door, up the steps, around the side of the house again and there was that same fair going on. I walked down the street again and I really felt free. People walked by and I smiled at them and even if they didn't smile back I didn't care. I walked back up the street and this time went through the front door, up a few flights of stairs, got back into bed again and I let myself go into a nice restful sleep.

People frequently ask us what hints we can give them so that they can begin to do this kind of work and see exactly how effective the results are. Here are several bits of advice.

Stories are constructed using the principle of parallelism or isomorphism, meaning that the critical elements of the story must have the same shape as the facts in the patient's life. This is done by matching in general terms, age, sex, family relations, perhaps occupation, etc., so that it paces the patient's unique situation. For instance, there are several appropriate metaphors for the family: a ship's captain, the first mate, and the crew; a school principal, the assistant principal and the teachers; the team coach, the assistant coach, and the players.

Next, be sure to use your own right hemisphere processes or creativity. Just go into your trance and generate an image or picture in your mind that is symbolic to you of the patient and the patient's situation. For example, a cigarette smoker might remind you of a machine that just is not running right; as a result of the malfunction there is too much friction between the gears and the machinery is smoking. Finally, a master engineer comes along and turns one particular screw in just the right way and after that the machine just runs quite efficiently and hums right along. A sad and lonely alcoholic patient might remind you of a forlorn puppy who would love to play with the other dogs in the neighborhood but just doesn't know how to go about doing that. Finally, a wise old St. Bernard comes along and helps the puppy out. The St. Bernard might whisper a wise secret into the puppy's ear. Or the St. Bernard might tell the puppy exactly what to do to be friendlier with the other dogs.

We would also advise you to find some friends or colleagues who are using or who are interested in using these approaches. It is sometimes difficult to think up stories by yourself; a professional support group meeting every few weeks to develop stories and metaphors for tough cases may prove invaluable, especially for beginners. This type of professional and personal brainstorming is also fun and helps prevent burnout and boredom.

The last piece of advice we offer is to remember that you must be congruent in all your behaviors for these therapeutic stories to work. We understand that it is risky for many professionals to do something different from what they were trained to do. Many people believe or fear that these stories or other indirect techniques will be embarrassingly obvious to the patient and that the patient will confront them with these facts. This has certainly not been our experience; however, we know that you have to trust your own experience and not our word. All we can tell you is that, if you would like to see how powerful and effective these techniques are, you have to try them. We often tell patients, "The only way to do it—is to do it!" Sitting around analyzing, processing, and hypothesizing about what may happen will not give you the sensory data needed to see how effective these techniques are. But again, they must be done in a powerful, effective, congruent way—as if you know they are going to work—for them to work.

Ironically, it is important for the professional to help the patient to forget the messages given indirectly. Since the point of indirect communication is that it addresses the right brain or unconscious, the last thing you would like is for the patient to leave your office consciously analyzing the techniques used or stories told, trying to consciously come up with a message. That is why embedded in many of our hypnotic inductions are forgetting messages.

> You, know, Frank, memory is a funny thing. It is something we value highly in this culture; in fact, as a health professional I think we overvalue it. Now I know you have a good memory, Frank. You remembered to come here today, and so did I – that's how we got together; it wasn't an accident. I know, Frank, if I ask you what you had for dinner last night, you could tell me quite easily. But think how difficult, how almost impossible it would be for you to tell me what you had for dinner one month ago. You've forgotten. Yet, believe it or not, that memory is somewhere inside of you. And if you ever needed to remember, you would be able to; but remembering what you had for dinner a month ago last night would just clog up your conscious mind and prevent it from doing other important work. You'll be happy to know, Frank, that the kind of work we are going to be doing here in this office is the same kind of material. Whatever you need to remember of our work, in whatever way you need to remember it – specifically or in great detail, or vaguely and hardly at all, you'll be able to remember it. When there are things said here that you don't need to remember, that would just be clogging up your mind like trying to remember what you had for dinner one month ago last night, you won't bother remembering it. You'll forget. And that's one of the nice things about the work we are going to do together.

In addition to implanting forgetting messages, with which most hypnotherapists should be familiar, it is important to remember not to consciously process this material with the patient. You need to trust your clinical work and wait a week or two to see what happens. We have seen beginning students of indirect communication tell beautiful stories or use elegant indirect communication techniques and then not trust it and immediately explain to the patient what they meant. The indirect communication then becomes nothing more than a parallel example for the patient to consciously mull over. Resist the temptation to explain everything you do to your patient. Trust your own work and expand your own creativity as you experiment with some of these new techniques.

CHAPTER 5

DIRECT COMMUNICATION

AUTHORS DISCUSSING MODERN hypnosis invariably find themselves locked on the horns of the dilemma of direct versus indirect communication, with most current practitioners showing a decided preference for the indirect (Yapko, 1983).

Indeed, early hypnotic interventions had, as their trademark, a standard induction followed by hypnotic suggestions directly phrased, such as "the sight of cigarettes will make you nauseated." Most people who desire hypnotherapy generally harbor the belief that this technique will provide the "fast and easy" way to diet, stop smoking or give up alcohol. The lay hypnotist and the media, as well as some professionals, share some responsibility for this. They promote the expectation that hypnotherapy involves induction of trance followed by direct suggestions that bring about rapid and enduring behavioral change. In fact, enough people *do* make substantial changes during group hypnotic sessions in motel and hotel conference rooms to give these hypnotists credibility (but then, one only need look at the lines of people buying lottery tickets to realize how little is needed in the way of reinforcement when the stakes are high).

Many beginning students, having learned induction methods, press us for specific posthypnotic suggestions for a variety of problems, including overeating, smoking, and alcoholism. Erickson's great wisdom was demonstrated in his understanding of the natural resistance of adults to follow direct suggestions from other adults. Most of us have had experience with children who are similarly disinclined to "do as they're told." Erickson's indirect, non-authoritarian, naturalistic approach was a major

advance in the field of hypnosis (Lankton and Lankton, 1983).

The emphasis on indirection has led to some confusion, however, and has, unfortunately, discredited direct communication. It is important to be able to pace those patients who will respond better to direct suggestions. Students of Erickson's techniques are frequently surprised when they first view his actual work. For example, in the videotape presentation, *The Artistry of Milton H. Erickson, M.D.* (Lustig, 1975), Erickson directs Monde as follows: " . . . close your eyes and feel that discomfort, knowing you can control it by opening your eyes. And now *first you feel* it thoroughly, the most uncomfortable feeling you've ever had; close your eyes and feel it . . . " *(Monde closes eyes)*. First-time viewers of Erickson's work usually do not expect him to make such direct suggestions. However, his interventions need to be understood in the context of the already established cooperative relationship, which is the nature of trance work. These direct suggestions and requests were being given for the purpose of teaching Monde a strategy to deal with the difficult events in her life by closing her eyes and then re-opening them.

We share Erickson's reservations about direct hypnotic suggestion, specifically about its usefulness for the abolition of symptoms, where the likelihood of success is small and the failure to achieve direct abolition of the symptom may have the undesirable effect of discrediting hypnotherapy as a useful tool (Erickson, 1978). Even so, direct communication does have its place in modern clinical hypnosis. The discussion of direct versus indirect communication—as if one were good or one were bad, one desired and one undesirable—clearly falls into the age-old trap of dichotomous thinking so characteristically reflected in mind/body duality or nature/nurture controversies. We consider it more useful to think of communication techniques as occupying a continuum; in any given case a particular technique—direct or indirect—may or may not be useful, depending on the specifics of the individual and the situation. As we move from a dichotomous, discontinuous categorization to a more fluid one, the unique role of directives comes into play. Directives are a form of direct communication which has its desired effect at both the conscious and unconscious (or indirect) level. *Our bot-*

tom line is effectiveness. All of what we do is designed with this goal in mind. A treatment program designed with this goal in mind may include direct and/or indirect approaches. Dogmatic adherence to one or another is a disservice to our patients.

So far we have introduced the concept of direct communication and suggested its usefulness as part of modern clinical hypnosis. In the rest of this chapter we will focus first on forms of direct communication and then describe a special subset, directives. *The common denominator of direct communications is that they are intended to be understood on the conscious level.*

THE USE OF NAMES

A successful hypnotic intervention is rapport-dependent; moreover, the hypnotic relationship is defined by its cooperative nature. We seek to maximize cooperation at the beginning of our clinical work by using the following strategy at the beginning of the first session: "Hello, I'm Gerry Bush. Would you like me to call you Ruth or Mrs. Louis?" The patient will then respond in one of two ways: "Call me Ruth" or "I prefer to be called Mrs. Louis." Or she might say, "Neither. My friends call me 'Ruthie' and and I prefer that."

Several important things occur in this brief interchange. By avoiding the use of professional titles ("I am Dr. X"), we offer our patients the opportunity to choose how they will address us, either by first name or by professional title and last name, since indeed they are all aware of our professional degrees. (Interestingly, our experience is that, when given the choice, a high percentage of patients do use our professional title.)

Asking how a patient likes to be addressed is a simple matter and perhaps seems too obvious to mention. However, we believe this to be an easy, respectful step toward building the relationship which is necessary for all psychotherapeutic work, especially hypnotic work. Indeed, the personalization of trance work by interspersing the individual's name frequently throughout the hypnotic inductions and utilization is critical to effective pacing.

An unpublished study conducted at Iowa State University

provides some interesting information on this point. The researchers were curious about the difference between the professional and lay population ratings of therapeutic effectiveness. Six freshmen psychology students (representing a lay population) and six members of the Iowa Psychological Association observed and rated 36 videotaped interactions. The interactions were set up as follows: Six patients were each interviewed by five skilled therapists and one graduate psychology student taking his first practicum course, who was included as a lark. The interaction consisted of the patient's making a statement and the therapist's responding briefly.

The study revealed no difference between the ratings of the lay and professional groups. More careful analysis revealed that not only was there no difference but that both groups rated one particular therapist significantly higher. It turned out that the highly rated therapist was the practicum student. Intrigued, the investigators then performed a content analysis in an effort to determine why both the freshmen psychology students and practicing psychologists rated this individual so highly. The only significant difference was that this individual invariably used the patient's name once, if not twice, in the brief response.

LANGUAGE NUANCES

We earlier discussed some of the lessons which the split brain studies (Springer and Deutsch, 1981) have taught us regarding hemispheric differentiation. At this point it might be useful to review the left brain/right brain metaphors that guide us in understanding how to formulate our interventions linguistically. No where has the subject been more eloquently explained than in Paul Watzlawick's *The Language of Change* (1978). In Chapter VI, entitled "Right Hemispheric Language Patterns," he discusses a critical feature of right hemispheric language, here referred to as figurative language:

> Finally, yet another property of figurative language must be mentioned. As already pointed out, its structure is comparatively primitive. It lacks the highly

developed logical syntax of digital communication (left hemispheric or natural language), above all the concept of "negation" — that is, words like *not, none, nobody, never, nowhere* and etc., which are indispensable for the direct expression of the notions of non-existence, absence, non-applicability and the like. As explained elsewhere . . . it is difficult, if not impossible, to represent the non-occurrence of an event by a picture. The sentence, *The man plants a tree*, can be rendered easily by a simple drawing but not its opposite (*The man does not plant a tree*). Whichever way one may try this meaning cannot be communicated unambiguously. Depending on the graphic solution attempted, one arrives at appropriate meanings like *A man beside a hole in the ground and an uprooted tree, Man and fallen tree* or something of that kind. Experienced hypnotists therefore avoid negations and replace them, wherever possible, by positive formulations (p. 66–67).

In general, the language of the right brain is more primitive than left hemispheric language and reflects primary process; as such it is without negation, tense, or mood (injunctive or subjunctive), and is represented metaphorically, iconographically and analogically. Using hemispheric differentiation and the model of trance as a predominately right brain experience, we generally avoid negation as countertherapeutic. The unconvinced may wish to consider the familiar example: "Please don't think of a purple pig now." The imagery of a purple pig occurs since imaging is right hemispheric property and the "don't" drops out. However, this does not mean that we always avoid the use of the word "no." You will recall that in Chapter 3 on *Anchoring* we asked the patient to imagine herself saying "no" and feeling good about refusing to eat. Obviously, a person can imagine herself saying "no." On the other hand, we take precise advantage of the fact that negations drop out, as Milton Erickson did when he said to a hesitant patient, "Please don't go into trance just yet." Note that the use of "yet" further modifies and confuses

very important —

the direction while implying that trance is inevitable. The individual who is intent on not going into trance, however, hears in his conscious mind a message that paces his desire not to enter trance. As a general guideline, hypnotic language should be stated so that the left and right brain representations are in harmony. For example, it is preferable to say "you will eat only helpful foods in the appropriate amount," rather than "you will not eat too much."

Many of our patients up the ante by blaming themselves for failing and not controlling the symptom. Not only do they hate themselves for being fat but also feel weak for failing at losing weight. Actually, the hidden clues come from our examination of the right brain language patterns in which the statement made to oneself "I won't eat" becomes a continually running injunction, which forces the right brain representation of eating to the front of the mind. In order to break this created obsession with food, the patient must eat and then the cycle rages again (Fisch, Weakland, and Segal, 1982).

"Try" is a word to be used with care in trance work. Inasmuch as this work depends on communication to both the right and left hemispheres we sometimes avoid the word "try," a "fail" word implying that success may not occur.

Therapist: "You wish to stop smoking. What approaches have you already used?"

Patient: "Well, I've tried cold turkey but that was awful because I started getting nervous. I've tried that system where you use the filters and decrease the amount of smoke that gets in and that didn't work. Then I switched to low tar cigarettes but found I was smoking more of them."

Therapist: "It sounds like you've had a difficult and unrewarding experience. When I listen to you, it seems clear to me that you need to know that no one's lungs ever got healthier from *trying* to quit, so I think you'd be pleased to know that hypnosis will help you to engage in healthier patterns."

On the other hand, "try" can be very useful when the therapist wishes to communicate failure. For example, in a hypnotic induction, when desiring eye closure and wishing to promote this indirectly, the hypnotist might say: "As you sit there listening to my voice, please try not to let your eyes close . . . try to keep your eyes open as long as you can."

Taking advantage of the linking words inherent in subordinate clauses, many hypnotic formulations are based on a "when/then" foundation. Indeed, this is the structure of the posthypnotic suggestion: "and when you say 'no' to that piece of cake, then you'll feel good about yourself" (see Chapter 3). Another example is: "And when your eyes close, then you can take yourself in your imagination to a favorite place. . . . "

 Note the inherent positiveness and inevitability implied by "when," a word we invariably use in place of "if." For example, discussing the achievement of a goal, we might say, "And when you stop smoking you may wonder about the ways you'll be feeling healthier both physically and psychologically."

LABELS

One of the keystones of our approach is the classic six-step reframing (see Chapter 6). This process provides the patient with an opportunity to generate alternative behavior patterns that can be substituted for the dysfunctional patterns which are labeled as symptomatic. The theoretical concept behind reframing is that the symptom which the patient understands as a sign of illness or weakness has a function. We can be respectful of the positive intent of the symptom or habit and utilize that to create an alternative reality which is more acceptable. Reframing takes the same (symptomatic) behavior and places it in a new context (frame), thereby providing a way to understand and accept the symptom in a way that enables change to occur. When the symptom is labeled "not a symptom," the patient's habitual patterns or struggles with himself or herself about the symptom are interrupted.

There is another use of the term reframing which, to avoid confusion, can be referred to as *relabeling*. This describes those communications which seek to promote change by enabling the individual to spontaneously experience himself differently through changing the *meaning* of something associated with him. For example, a patient who complains about <u>being overly dependent</u> <u>on the opinions of others</u> can have that behavior relabeled as <u>sensitivity in interpersonal relationships.</u>

words !

It is often helpful to relabel words to which individual patients have developed negative connotations. For example, many patients seem to be "allergic" to <u>the word "exercise."</u> While it would be dysfunctional to stress to them the importance of exercise, it can be very helpful to discuss an *increase in everyday activity* as part of the weight control program. Likewise, we find many patients respond better to the notion of "<u>healthy eating patterns</u>" than to that dreaded word, "<u>diet.</u>"

ELICITING QUESTIONS

Imagine that your patient, Jan, is having difficulty incorporating an exercise regime into his program for weight management. <u>Using the telephone technique described in Chapter 4,</u> you wait until Jan is in the office at the beginning of his next appointment and then, in a somewhat distracted or discombobulated manner, you excuse yourself, pick up the phone and <u>call your receptionist.</u> You ask, "When is Pat coming in? (pause) Oh, good. I want to remember to tell her about that new exercise regime. I believe it will be very helpful to her." <u>Should you work without a receptionist, the local weather lady can come in handy.</u> Your conversation would be a little different: "I have to make a quick call, please excuse me." After dialing the weather, say, "Department of Physiology, please. I'd like to speak to Dr. Jones." Having waited an appropriate amount of time, you continue, "Dr. Jones, this is Dr. Smith. I wanted to thank you for the <u>activity program</u> you described. One of my patients, who has had a problem with being overweight and couldn't find an appropriate program, has already reported some satisfying success with your activity program."

You already know that this has been a difficult area for Jan; further, he has already told you that people have given him lots of unsolicited and unappreciated advice. <u>Using this method, the trick is to provide him with the opportunity and motivation to</u> *ask you* <u>for the information, breaking the pattern of rejecting spontaneously-offered advice.</u>

If Jan takes the bait, you might preface your response to Jan's query with a comment such as the following, offered sympathetically of course, "I'm not sure this would be right for you. In fact, you have told me how much difficulty you have had in the past with exercise." In all likelihood this will cause Jan to intensify his requests. In presenting the program, with your doubts fully but sympathetically expressed (the rule of congruence forbids sarcasm here), you are challenging Jan to prove you wrong and to adopt an exercise regimen.

PARALLEL EXAMPLES

Parallel stories are simply examples whose structure is similar or identical to the structure of the patient's problem situation, yet removed enough so the patient can listen somewhat nondefensively. The major difference between this direct technique and the indirect technique of metaphors previously discussed is that the connection is pointed out explicitly to the patient. One such parallel example is as follows:

> You know, Leslie, when I was a child I grew up in New York City near the Bronx Park. I used to play with my friend Janet on the rocks in that part of the park near the zoo. We played carefully and with a great deal of excitement because the cliffs were so high and treacherous. This was one of the most exciting things that we did together and probably the most dangerous. Our parents would watch us carefully and caution us not to run too fast for fear that we would fall. When my family moved away from the city, I remembered with a shiver of excitement our daring escapades on the rocks. A number of years later, I happened to be back in the old neighborhood and found myself wandering around some of the places where I had grown up. I was surprised to see how insignificant the "cliffs" were. They were barely over six feet high. You know, Leslie, it's interesting that many times in our lives we find ourselves faced with an enormous task ahead of us only to find that it turns

out to be much less of an obstacle once we get some
new perspectives. And the same may be true about
you and your problem with alcohol.

This story can be told while the patient is in or out of trance
or as part of the trance induction. Another example of a parallel
story germane to habit disorders is the friendly enemy story
told in Chapter 4 (see p. 76).

Another parallel example is specific to individuals who overeat. Since many left hemispheric processes are not yet well developed we believe that children spend a lot of time in trance
 during the first several years of life; we might, therefore, consider the following story as a means to reverse childhood hypnosis. A parallel example can be an effective way of breaking
unquestioned beliefs:

> When you were young, your mother and father
> told you many things which, as a child, you believed
> to be true because you had no reason to believe they
> weren't. After all, parents are always right—at least
> that's what a small child is taught. But as you grew
> older, you learned, at least in some areas, that your
> parents did not have all the answers. I don't know if
> it was in the area of love and sex and dating or per-
> haps in the area of current events or politics, but like
> most of us you had the experience of finding out that
> they were off the mark sometimes. And it would be
> interesting, wouldn't it, if one of the times they were
> wrong was when they told you that "all gone is good."
> The fact is, the food that you can't see at the end of
> a meal is the food that can hurt you. What you see
> on your plate can't become extra weight.

IDENTIFICATION WITH ANOTHER

Milton Erickson's problem-solving approach appears to be
based on his understanding of hypnosis as a tool to connect
people with their inner resources. We sometimes find that some

patients seem to be unaware of, and unable to access, their resources and all the things that they have experienced and learned
in life, claiming they are unable to do what is asked of them.
Less frequently, we see patients who have led particularly im-
poverished lives and lack past experience to learn from and rely
upon. This might become evident when a homework assignment
is given or when the individual is faced with what he or she feels
is a particularly arduous task.

"I don't think that I can say that to my mother,"
said Ralph when told he needed to say "no" to her invitations to come home for the excessive meals which
had led to his weight problem.

Since a strong therapist-patient relationship had
already been established over several sessions, the
therapist replied, "You're right, you are unable to
stand up to your mother, even though you told me
that would be an important step for you to control
your overeating. And you know that I could do that
quite easily and comfortably, so why don't you just
imagine that you're me. After all, you know more
about me than you may consciously realize. I wonder
if you'd be willing to just close your eyes for a moment
and, after taking a few deep breaths, think about just
how I'd say what I would say and how I would say
it. That's right. And you might wonder just how your
mother would react and you might notice how confused she would be when you handled this expertly
and appropriately."

At this juncture it would be appropriate to model
some satisfactory statements that Ralph might make
which would be therapeutic and non-inflammatory.
"Perhaps I would say, 'I appreciate your invitations
and know that you want to feed me and nurture me.
I will seek to come home more frequently as long as
you cook appropriate meals. However, if you should
continue to make excessive meals and demand that
I eat them, I'm going to have no choice but not to

come. So you can see the amount of visiting that we
have together is really based on what you do.'"

The patient may discover someone else with whom to identify. This may be a real person or a fictional character. It would
then be important for the therapist to explore with the patient
what this other individual would say in the given situation to
be sure it is not inflammatory and remains therapeutic. Again,
the basic idea is for the therapist to help the patient imagine
in some detail what this other person would do in the given situation and then instruct him to go out and do it.

DIRECT SUGGESTIONS FOR IMAGERY

Sometimes we find it helpful, especially to increase motivation, to give patients direct suggestions to produce specific imagery.

For instance, when a woman patient expressed concern about
her appearance in a social context, we directed her to imagine
herself the following summer at her goal weight in a fashionable
bathing suit on a beach she had visited and enjoyed before. We
asked her to notice particularly the positive reactions she was
getting from the other people on the beach.

Or, we might ask a patient to see himself in a mirror as he
looks today. Then the patient is asked to turn the mirror around
and to magically see himself as he looks at his goal weight and
to be aware of how good he feels about that.

There has been much written concerning the use of hypnosis
and aversive suggestions. Whenever possible, we prefer to use
positive imagery rather than negative scare tactics. We have
simply found that a majority of patients respond much more
favorably to being told how good they will feel when they are
in control of the situation rather than to being asked to imagine negative stimulation such as a skull and crossbones on a cigarette pack. Of course, as discussed in detail in Chapter 2, we
are always willing to pace patient's needs and beliefs. Some patients, for whatever reasons, respond better to aversive suggestions, and so it is important that the therapist be flexible enough
to use such suggestions when appropriate.

As an example of such a utilization, one of the authors was treating an ex-combat veteran for smoking. The patient stated, "You're going to have to really scare me and hit me hard for this to work Doc." During the session, it was suggested to the patient that he imagine seeing a cigarette as a bullet and that he would remember that picture. On follow-up one year later, the patient reported that he had abstained from smoking and that the suggestion to see a cigarette as a bullet was what had helped him most.

DIRECTIVES

Directives are a unique subset or form of direct communication. Unlike most of the techniques presented previously in this chapter, the goal of which is to help change attitudes or motivate the patient, directives are specific instructions given by the therapist that require particular behaviors, which have been designed to promote a desirable therapeutic outcome. Watzlawick (1985) has made a central distinction between most psychotherapies and Ericksonian hypnotherapy. He states that the former are characterized by *descriptive* language (the language of insight), and the latter by *injunctive* language. Watzlawick describes as "hypnotherapy without trance" the use of those "linguistic structures which have a virtually hypnotic effect without the use of trance." He points out that all of hypnosis is characterized by the words "do this." We believe that directives in and of themselves can perform the same function as hypnosis. In a similar vein, Haley has stated that the fundamental nature of hypnosis is that an individual is instructed to do something, at the same time he is not to do anything at all: "Your hand will rest on your lap, and you will not move it, but by itself it will begin to rise up in the air and touch your face . . . " (Haley, 1963).

Earlier, we made an oversimplified distinction between direct and indirect communication, commenting on the obvious deficiencies in such dichotomous distinctions (one of the pitfalls of the left hemispheric analytic model). Stepping out of the limited framework of *either* direct *or* indirect, we become able to perceive the large "excluded middle." We can then consider the notion that *both* direct *and* indirect communications occur simultaneously (Stolzenberg, 1984). In this fascinating middle ground lies a group of interventions called directives. On a theoretical level, directives are statements or instructions to the patient, telling him or her directly to do one thing or another. So that the patient will carry out these instructions, the therapist must provide a rationale that is consistent with the patient's frame of reference and makes sense to the patient. However, the indirectness lies in the fact that the directive is frequently constructed in such a way that the patient is unaware that the performance of the directive will entail a shift in behavior. This will move the person out of a generally locked-in position. Once he follows the directive his frame of reference changes and new possibilities become apparent.

Generally, patients are seen in therapy one hour a week and spend the remaining 111 hours of their week in the context of their everyday activities. (Note that we are assuming eight hours of sleep a day; an insomniac has even more non-therapy hours available!) Therefore, in addition to the interventions, hypnotic or otherwise, which are used in the office, we invariably give directives as homework assignments to be done between sessions, since we are seeking behavioral change in the context of the patient's life, not in the context of a one-hour-a-week therapy session.

Directives, as we use them, fall into five basic categories: 1) informational directives, 2) directives to be used for screening or for mobilization of the patient's potential, as well as for defining the therapist's control of the situation, 3) metaphoric directives, 4) directives for self-hypnosis, and 5) directives which block attempted solutions.

Informational Directives

This class of directives is most applicable to individuals who are overweight, and who, we therefore assume, are overeating. The goal for these individuals is to modify their eating habits (this is rarely the case with smoking or drinking, where the goal usually is to totally abolish the habit). We have found that it is often a mistake to assume that people are aware of proper

Q. what is "normal"

eating habits. Consequently, we strongly recommend that, during the initial interview, the clinician obtain a <u>very detailed description of the circumstances of each meal or snack</u>. This would include the time of day, place, the presence or absence of other individuals, the period of time spent eating, precisely what is eaten and whether the individual is engaged in any other activity, such as reading, writing, watching television, listening to music or conversing. For many individuals, <u>dysfunctional eating habits relate to the fact that eating has become an unconscious activity.</u> As you pursue this line of questioning, you may learn that the patient lives alone, watches television very often, and takes only ten minutes to eat. If this is the case, it would be appropriate to give some directives which would seek to modify these behaviors. Such directives would clearly be informational in type, but they may be given in such a way as to secure compliance. For example, one might say the following:

> Sylvia, it sounds as if a lot of your eating is automatic. I am concerned that you have not been providing your body with an opportunity to be aware of the physiologic processes that occur when you eat. This may be related to the difficulty in not knowing when you've eaten enough. Therefore, I'd like you to test out this hypothesis in the following way. Number one, I would like you to <u>turn off the television when you</u> eat; number two, <u>cut your food in small pieces;</u> and number three, <u>chew each piece eight times</u>, savoring the flavor and texture, and <u>swallow slowly</u>. I would like you to pay attention to the feelings of fullness, and stop eating when you are comfortably full.

As you can see, the directive is framed as a way to check out the level of body awareness and, at the same time, to increase body awareness. If an individual would follow such directions given purely as information, it would not be necessary to go through such an elaborate rigamarole. However, in our experience, overweight people have been given lots of advice on how to eat and are usually unlikely to follow such direct suggestions.

When the clinician is sure that the patient is a cooperative patient, there is obviously no reason to avoid giving suggestions directly.

Screening and Motivational Directives

In Chapter 8, we will discuss the fact that it is important for the clinician to avoid treating people who are not motivated to change, but who present themselves because of the encouragement or pressure of friends or family members. It is usually easy to detect those who have really come to you for help because those persons will display a sincere desire to be relieved of their symptoms. Nevertheless, it can be useful to use a directive as a screening device. This is also a way to indicate that the therapist is in control of the situation and thus assure compliance with further directives.

> For example, one of us received a call from a woman who complained of being overweight and depressed. In the course of the initial interview, the woman described herself as being powerless and unable to do anything in her life. In order to indicate that therapy was going to be focused on action rather than words, a directive was employed. The therapist had learned that this woman, using various diets, had lost and regained 40 pounds on several different occasions. At the end of the initial interview she was instructed to go home and lose 10 pounds. When she had done so she should call for a second appointment, and then the therapy would proceed.
>
> The rationale for this directive was twofold. First, toward the end of the initial session, the therapist was still not clear in his own mind as to the source of the patient's motivation. Friends were "pushing" her to get help and her perceived passive-dependent/passive-aggressive personality style may have required her to "try and fail." Secondly, this patient was a tough fighter for control, but in inappropriate situations.

For example, the patient presented many difficulties regarding the scheduling of the first appointment, even though she was not working and appeared to be available any day. On the other hand, this patient did not take control of situations where it was appropriate for her to do so (i.e., control her food intake).

The directive enabled the therapist to gain control of the therapy situation by forcing the patient to follow his directive before therapy would begin. It also forced the patient to begin to assert her control over her eating habits. The patient was very angry about the situation and did not commit herself to follow the directive or to continue therapy. She called ten days later and said that she had lost nine plus pounds and was "a few grams shy" of the stipulated ten pounds. When she asked for an appointment, she was told that the conditions were ten pounds exactly and that it was certain to only be a few more days until she had lost the entire ten pounds and would be ready to call again.

In this instance, the therapist would have made a grave error in acceding to the patient's wish for an appointment after only nine plus pounds of weight loss. The patient would have proved that she could control the terms of treatment – but not necessarily her own weight. The therapist must be in control of the treatment, either overtly or covertly. Being a patient's "friend" is seldom the most expeditious way to effect change.

When discussing directives, the issue of manipulation again rears its head. We believe it is useful to focus on the fact that people come to therapy because they want to make changes, although they don't know how to do so. If they were able to change on their own, they would not need to seek help. Consequently, the therapist's role is to promote change, and the bottom line is how best to do that for a particular individual within a given set of circumstances. We understand that the word "manipulation" has negative connotations; perhaps the word "persuasion" might be more acceptable. In any event, we prefer to be effective. By the way, it should be noted that in the above example the therapist, dealing with a depressed woman who had asserted her powerlessness and inability to change, countered with an equally powerful position from which he did not deviate, even for the lack of a few grams. This indicated to the woman his belief that she had some resources which could be mobilized. Simply having the woman lose weight as a precondition of treatment becomes an implicit message that change is possible, and that, indeed, her description of herself as totally stuck in life is less than fully accurate.

Directives are an essential part of our therapy. They are usually given as homework at the end of a session. It is not uncommon for us to indicate to patients that we expect them to do their homework; we add that if they fail to do it, we will charge for their visit but not see them, and schedule another appointment only after the homework assignment has been completed. Consistent with this, each session begins with our checking on how the homework assignment was carried out. This also serves to screen out people who are more interested in talking about and gaining insight into their problem than in doing something about it. We usually refer such individuals to another psychotherapist.

As we mentioned earlier, if the patient is to follow the directive, he needs to be given some logical reason for doing so. Often, in giving directives we use hypnosis as a motivational "carrot." For example, the patient described below needed to begin to change his eating habits, but it was apparent to the therapist that he did not need hypnosis in order to do that; rather, all he needed were some instructions regarding healthy dietary habits.

Les came for therapy weighing 300 pounds, saying that he had tried the Beverly Hills Diet, the Atkins Diet, and the Pritikin Diet. He had lost weight, as much as 100 pounds for a while on each one, but then unfortunately he gained it back. He came to us because he believed hypnosis would be the answer to his problem. Questioning Les about eating habits revealed that he ate only one meal a day, invariably in front of the television set, while reading or watching TV or both. He ate no formal meals at other times. He would often eat when he was around food, which occurred frequently since he was in the restaurant business.

Les was told that hypnosis would be very helpful to him, but that he was not yet ready for hypnosis. In order for hypnosis to be helpful, we said, he needed to change his eating habits dramatically. He was then given the same kind of information that was described in the section on informational directives: He would need to eat several regular meals a day and would have to eat without watching television or reading the newspaper and to concentrate on the sensory experiences of eating. When his habits had become regular (without, necessarily, a change in the amount of food eaten), he would then be ready for hypnosis.

By the time Les had reformed his eating habits, most of the necessary therapeutic change had already taken place. However, in such cases, in order to pace the person's belief that hypnosis is necessary for successful treatment of the weight problem, we do a few hypnotic intervention sessions as described in various parts of this book. This reinforces the good work the person is already doing and allows him or her to carry on with it after terminating treatment. Obviously, we never say to the patient that most of the work has been done without hypnosis; rather, we use his or her belief that we can help because we are "good hypnotists."

Metaphoric Directives

Metaphoric directives are especially interesting and allow for a certain amount of therapeutic creativity. It is one thing to tell an individual to get his life in order and quite another to direct him to go home and clean out his basement or attic.

A woman came in because of severe problems with overeating. During the initial evaluation, it became

clear that this patient's life was chaotic. After learning that much of the dysfunctional eating occurred
at home, the therapist asked the patient whether her
refrigerator had been cleaned out recently. When she
said, "no," the therapist gave her the following directive, using a rationale that dealt with the appropriate
issues for her:

"Ruth, in order for you to prepare yourself for the
task of modifying your eating habits, I'd like you to
spend some time, when you're all by yourself, reor-
ganizing and cleaning out your refrigerator. Now,
when they do this some people start at the top and
work their way down to the bottom. Other individuals start at the bottom and work their way up to the
top. Still others clear out the doors first and then
move on to the shelves of the refrigerator in whatever
order they choose to do. Other people simply take out
items at random. Now, some of the items that you
take out you are going to find are spoiled and need
to be discarded. Still others are fine just the way they
are, and there will probably be another group which
are OK but need to be rewrapped."

The purpose of such a directive is, of course, to get the individual to do something which she can see as a tangible step toward her goal. At the same time, the directive metaphorically
encourages the person to reorganize more than just the refrigerator.

Directives for Self-hypnosis

We prefer to present hypnotherapy in a way that debunks
the widely held notion that hypnosis involves "mind control" by
the hypnotist. Consequently, we explain to our patients that
trance is a natural ability that we all have and that part of the
therapist's role is to teach them how to use self-hypnosis, which
will be useful to them in resolving their problem themselves. Our
responsibility, therefore, is to teach them a skill, and though we

are proficient in teaching the skill, we cannot "do the work for them." Therefore, as part of the treatment contract, our patients agree at the very outset, to practice self-hypnosis at home between office visits. Consequently, the initial sessions in the office are often framed as "trance training." We explain to our patients that we will teach them a method of going into trance that will be satisfactory for them and then allow them to be in trance for the better part of the session. We explain that we will be talking to them and that what we will be saying will not be of particular significance, but will merely be "hypnotic patter," background "noise" to help them stay in their trance, and that they may or may not be aware of anything we say, but that it doesn't matter because it is not significant. This gives us a potentially fruitful space to tell therapeutic metaphors, because, after all, we have to fill in the time with "hypnotic patter."

After we have found an induction method which is comfortable for the individual, we give the suggestion, at the close of the first trance, that in order for him to go into trance in the future, when he is practicing at home, all he needs to do is repeat what took place in the office.

Using this approach, self-hypnosis becomes somewhat matter-of-fact. At first, we sometimes found that many patients believed that they hadn't learned "the real" self-hypnosis, because they expected, with self-hypnosis (as well as with "heterohypnosis"), that they should put themselves in trance and then tell themselves that they will not want to eat – or some other negative injunction. It is important to spend some time clarifying the conscious/unconscious dissociation which is at the root of hypnotic work. In general, all of us attempt to solve problems using conscious processes – logical and analytical ways to approach difficulties. When they work, of course, the problem is solved. However, the conscious mind is often limited by its preconceived beliefs. Hypnosis is a process that allows each of us to become connected with our unconscious mind, a repository of resources not ordinarily available. Therefore, hypnosis (and, of course, self-hypnosis) is an activity that allows the conscious mind to do whatever it needs to do while the unconscious mind begins to work on the problem. With that in mind, the procedure of self-hypnosis involves setting aside five, 10, or perhaps 15 minutes a day, or every other day, for the purpose of going into trance so that the unconscious mind can work on the problem area. In order to do this effectively, we instruct our patients as follows:

Frank, in order for you to continue to work on this problem you have with X, it will be important for you to practice self-hypnosis as we have discussed earlier. I would like you to get yourself situated in a place where you won't be disturbed, and remind yourself, consciously, that you are going to go into trance to allow your unconscious mind to provide you with some help in this problem area. Now I would like you to (*at this point you give the patient a detailed description, repeating the steps of the trance that you are using with this particular patient*). The mere act of being in trance will provide your unconscious mind with the opportunity to do some helpful things for you. It is important to know that your conscious mind may be involved in any sort of activity. It may be paying attention to various images, vague or distinct, or it may wander from image to image. You may have thoughts and you might wonder whether you are doing things quite correctly. On the other hand, you may be aware of sounds in the environment, or perhaps, you'll have no awareness whatsoever of what's going on around you and the immediate circumstances. But the very interesting thing is that it really doesn't matter what your conscious mind does, because the mere act of allowing yourself to go into trance will provide your unconscious with the opportunity to do what it knows how to do best. At the end of that five or 10 minutes, you will find yourself coming out of trance, and I suspect that you are liable to feel somewhat refreshed or comfortable, and certainly I expect that you will be quite satisfied with having taken the time and opportunity to provide yourself with this important experience.

Even though we see smokers for only one session, we still give them the strategy for using self-hypnosis. We tell patients the following:

> In this initial time period when you are seeking to consolidate changes in your behavior associated with ceasing to smoke, there may be a voice in your head which says, "It's OK to have a cigarette," "one won't hurt you," etc. As long as that voice keeps talking to you, you are vulnerable. As long as you give into that voice, even on an occasional basis, it will never stop telling you, "It's OK to have that cigarette," and you will eventually go back to smoking. It's critically important that you don't smoke at all so that the goal for the next several weeks is to have a strategy to deal with that voice that talks to you. Self-hypnosis is the appropriate way for you to respond to that voice. I would like to suggest that when that voice begins to talk to you and tell you, "It's OK," the way to quiet that voice down is to use it as a signal for you to practice self-hypnosis for the purpose of continuing your ever-increasing length of time without a cigarette.

a cue for auto-h.!

Directives Which Block Attempted Solutions

This class of directives seeks to have a direct therapeutic effect by addressing a very interesting notion – the notion developed over the last 20 years at the Mental Research Institute in Palo Alto that people's problematic behaviors are maintained by the very solutions they use in an attempt to solve the problem. This notion has been extensively described in the writings of the Mental Research Institute and is presented best in two volumes: *Change* (Watzlawick, Weakland, and Fisch, 1974) and *The Tactics of Change* (Fisch, Weakland, and Segal, 1982). The basic premise is that people make a logical error in approaching problems and this logical error maintains the interactional loop and perpetuates the problem. Therefore, in order to solve the patient's problem (chief complaint), the therapist must, in some way, block the attempted solution. Because the patient's problem-solving behavior is logical to him, it is frequently quite difficult to get him to stop what he is doing and do something else instead. Therefore, it is necessary to present the directive in a way that makes "logical" sense to the individual from his frame of reference, but has the desired effect of interrupting the repetitive cycle.

In *The Tactics of Change*, Fisch et al. describe the individual who has a problem with overeating. The patient's usual attempt to deal with this involves telling herself, "I won't eat, I will not eat, I won't overeat, I won't eat those foods," etc. From our earlier discussion in this chapter, it will be remembered that the "N" words ("no," "not") fall out of the right hemispheric representation of such statements. Consequently, the patient is repeating to her right brain, "I will eat, I do want to eat, I want those foods, etc." As a result, all she thinks about is *eating*; in order to break the obsessive pattern, she frequently gives in, which then stops the compulsive injunctions to eat, for the moment at least. At the same time, however, she feels guilty, and the cycle starts up again. The way to interrupt that cycle is shown in the following example.

Violet was 80 pounds overweight. During the initial intake, it was learned that she overate at four o'clock every day while at work. She described this in terms of "sabotaging herself." Violet said that this afternoon snack was the only time that the sabotaging occurred and talked in terms of eating candy bars or other unhealthy foods. She was asked what happened when she sabotaged herself; that is, was she aware of why it was that she sabotaged herself? She indicated that she was not. The therapist wondered aloud whether she felt guilty after sabotaging herself and because of that overwhelming feeling hadn't been able to become aware of what precipitated the sabotage in the first place. She indicated that, indeed, that was the case.

With this information, the therapist gave her a directive, which was labeled as something strange and curious, but something he thought would be helpful. He said to her, "In order for us to get control of your sabotaging, I would like you to do something that will get some more information about why you're sabotaging yourself. I would like you to deliberately set out to sabotage yourself at breakfast and lunch and be aware of any new insights about this. Can you tell me what you would do to sabotage your eating at that time?" She replied, "I would put extra butter on toast or a roll, or perhaps I would have cream sauce or cheese sauce on the vegetable at lunch time." She gave him a strange look, but acknowledged that she would follow the directive because she did wish to understand why she sabotaged herself.

She came back the next week and reported that, although the task was strange and didn't make sense, she performed it anyway. What was interesting was that she found that the sabotaging at four o'clock stopped by itself.

The therapist's covert goal was to stop the patient's four o'clock struggles. The directive was designed to do that by stopping the obsessive thought patterns. It was, however, presented in a way that was acceptable to the patient's belief about how change occurs (gaining insight into the cause of the problem). Let us emphasize that the therapist did not discuss the strategy or the results with the patient. In our experience, once the behavioral change occurs, most patients forget the originally described intent.

Many of you will identify this intervention as "symptom prescription." Indeed, this has been well documented as an effective way to get behavioral change. In the "interactional" view developed by the staff at the Mental Research Institute, the success of the intervention would be described in terms of her no longer struggling with herself about eating at four o'clock; that is, she no longer reminded herself that she should not eat at that time. Another explanation is that the symptom prescription enables the individual to gain control, to purposefully do something which in the past was labeled involuntary. The involuntary nature of the behavior is part of what makes it a "symptom."

This chapter has illustrated that the successful use of hypnosis for habit control includes non-hypnotic interventions as well. However, directives, as described in this chapter, have the same injunctive language as hypnosis and can therefore be thought of as "hypnotherapy without trance."

CHAPTER 6

REFRAMING

THE HEART OF THE modern hypnotic approach to the treatment of habit disorders is the technique called *reframing*. Reframing assumes that an unhealthy pattern of behavior has secondary gains—that it benefits the person in some way or ways—and treatment takes this into account. To understand reframing better, we now invite you to work on your own unhealthy habit or compulsive pattern of behavior by following these instructions for reframing:

Take a few deep breaths of air, make yourself comfortable, and take a few moments of time to identify the pattern of behavior that you wish to change. Let us call that pattern X. X may be something that you wish to stop or modify in some way, such as smoking, or X may be something that you wish to do or begin to do, such as writing a dissertation, but something is stopping you.

Now that you have identified X, the next step of reframing is to establish communication with that "part" of you that, in the past, has been responsible for X. We have found that very often this part of the person responsible for X has been, for the most part, an unconscious part of you. If that is the case, we would like to ask that part of you to now make itself known, in some safe way, to your unconscious. Please take a few moments of time and go into your own mind—wherever you have to go—and become aware of that part of you that, in the past, has been respon-

sible for X.* Now, we don't know exactly how you'll
experience that part of you that has been responsible
for X. It may be a familiar type of experience or a
unique one. It may be something you'll see in your
own mind: It can be any kind of visual image at all.
For example, you may see a color, or you may see an
object or a face. Your experience of that inner part
of you may be some kind of auditory experience, for
example a voice – perhaps even your own – or somebody else's voice or some other sound. Your experience of that part of you that was responsible for X
in the past may be a feeling of some kind. Please go
into your own mind now and become aware of that
part of you. We respectfully ask that that part of you
allow itself to be experienced in some kind of safe,
comfortable way by your consciousness.

There may be many of you who did not become

---

*This awareness, as well as carrying out further instructions in this section, is
facilitated by hypnotic trance. Therefore, any reader versed in self-hypnosis may
choose to go into trance at such time.

aware of any particular experience which could be identified as an awareness of that part of you that was responsible for X. Even if you haven't had such an experience, please proceed with the understanding that your unconscious may just not feel comfortable with your experiencing what we have suggested and that's all right. If you have experienced that part of you that has been responsible for X, we would like to thank that part of you for the communication, and we suggest that you might also wish to thank that part.

We would like to let that part of you that was responsible for X in the past know that we very much respect that part of you. That part of you is obviously very powerful, because even though you have wanted to change or modify X in the past, you haven't been able to do so. Therefore, we understand that this part of you that's been responsible for X will only change X as soon as it's ready to do so.

We would now like to suggest to you that, in some kind of way, X has had benefits or payoffs for you in the past. We understand that the actual experience or behavior of X has caused negative or unhealthy consequences for you, but we are suggesting that you now *reframe* your understanding of X to realize that *the intention of X has been to help or to benefit you.*

Now, take a few moments of time and go into your mind and become aware of what the payoffs or benefits of X have been for you. Has X helped get something that some part of you has desired or wanted (e.g., attention from your family)? Has X helped you to avoid something that would be uncomfortable or painful (e.g., intimacy)? Again, we are asking you to assume that X has continued up to now because it has helped you out or benefited you in some way. So, please become aware, if it is safe and comfortable enough to have this awareness, of how X has helped you.

Now, keeping the payoff or payoffs of X in mind, we would like to suggest that available to you are alternative patterns of behavior, experiencing, or perception that can provide whatever payoffs or benefits X provided you in the past. However, these new patterns of behavior would be healthier and perhaps even more satisfying to you. Would you now take some moments of time and go into your mind again. Tap into the creative resources of your mind and allow it to generate for you alternative patterns of behavior that you can substitute for X that will give you the same payoffs as X but be healthier for you.

Now that you have constructed alternative patterns of behavior, the next step of reframing is to do an *ecological check*. This means that you will check out these new alternatives with that part of you that was responsible for X in the past to make sure that that part of you, as well as all parts of you, will be comfortable and satisfied with the new alternatives. Would you now go into your mind again and make sure that your new alternatives seem all right, sound all right, and feel all right to that part of you that was responsible for X and to all parts of you.

If you receive a "no" signal, or in some way experience incongruence from any part of you (e.g., an increase in tension or irritability), in response to your new alternatives, then it is necessary for you to return to a prior step of reframing. For example, you may need to go back and allow your creative part to generate a new alternative or alternatives. Or you may have to go even further back and identify and take into account some payoff that you were not aware of before. If your new alternatives check out, then the next step of reframing is what is called *future pacing*. Please go into your mind and imagine yourself in the future to several of the next times and places when you have exhibited X in the past. Imagine that, instead, you now use or know that you have available to you the new alternative patterns of behavior that you have just become aware of. Imagine yourself in these future contexts with the new alternatives. If you experience significant difficulty, it may be necessary for you to generate more suitable alternatives. After you have successfully imagined future contexts with alternative patterns of behavior, you have completed the process of reframing.

We would now like to suggest that you appreciate the communication that has just taken place with your unconscious. We, the authors, very much appreciate any healthy work that you may have just completed and we thank you for the communication that we have just had with you. We also understand that you may not be *consciously* aware of any work that has taken place. However, we have found that just by reading about reframing, healthy unconscious processes are often set into motion. We've also discovered that, quite often, while a person is working on "X," "Y" and "Z" are being worked on as well.

The words you've just read are very similar to what we use in communicating to our patients during a reframing. In actual clinical situations, of course, we would modify our communication to pace or establish rapport with a particular patient. In clinical situations, a reframing might take anywhere from just a few minutes in one clinical session to dozens of clinical hours over many months. For example, sometimes a patient may need help and support over several sessions just to become aware of the payoffs of an unhealthy habit.

Here are the six basic steps of reframing:

1) Identify the habit or compulsive pattern of behavior (X) to be changed.

2) Establish communication with that part of the patient that has been responsible for X.

3) Suggest to the patient that the behavior of X be separated from the *positive intention* of the part responsible for X. In other words, X has had payoffs or benefits for the patient.
4) Suggest that the patient generate new behaviors that provide the needed payoffs.
5) Do an "ecological check." Are the alternative patterns of behavior acceptable to all parts of the person?
6) Future pace. Check out the alternative patterns of behavior within relevant future contexts.

The processes involved in reframing are facilitated by hypnotic trance. Trance heightens inner awareness and therefore helps the patient to become aware of inner "parts" and of payoffs from an unhealthy habit. Trance is a bridge to unconscious resources and potentials and thus aids the patient in constructing healthier alternatives. Because trance facilitates the imagination and breaks down the subjective barriers of past and future, the future pacing step of reframing is also facilitated. However, in using reframing, we have found no relationship between depth of trance and successful outcomes. In fact, we have worked with many patients who displayed no significant signs of trance during reframing but who still greatly benefited from the procedure.

Reframing accounts for the secondary gains or payoffs present with any habitual disorder. These payoffs are frequently disregarded by many health professionals and clinical hypnotists, who often rely simply on suggesting or lecturing to the patient about the unhealthy aspects of a habit. In such instances, the professional forgets that the patient has heard this lecture thousands of times already and that telling him again just generates more resistance to change.

The nice thing about reframing is that it is so "respectful" of the patient and his behaviors. By communicating an understanding that the destructive habit has actually been *helping* the patient, resistance is defused. Instead of fighting with the patient, as so many other people have done already, the health professional is able through reframing to "ally" himself with the patient or the patient's resistance. Patients often find this approach surprising and refreshing, which tends to open up many new doors to health and growth. Another elegant aspect of reframing is that *most of the work is left up to the patient*, not the health professional. Reframing utilizes the patient's own inner power and resources to construct alternative patterns of behavior. Patients appreciate this and feel better about themselves, as well as more powerful, after the work is completed.

The remainder of this chapter will elaborate upon each step of reframing and describe forms of reframing other than the six-step technique.

IDENTIFYING THE HABIT TO BE CHANGED

In most clinical situations, following this first step is easy. The patient desires to stop smoking cigarettes, to stop over-eating, or to stop ingesting alcohol. However, a patient will often request work on two or more unhealthy habits at the same time (this is especially true for smoking and overeating, and to a lesser degree for alcohol abuse and smoking). We strongly recommend not working on changing two unhealthy habits at the same time for several reasons. First of all, the payoffs are often different and the work becomes confusing. Secondly, it is often difficult enough for a patient to give up or modify *one* habitual pattern of behavior that has been relied upon for a long time (many years in most cases). We consider it insensitive to work on giving up or modifying two habits at the same time, and to do so greatly increases the probability of treatment failure.

When a patient asks for work on two unhealthy habits, you should first help the patient to identify the easier habit to change or modify and proceed with that work. After the patient has successfully engaged in new and healthier patterns of behavior instead of the first habit for a few months, then the second unhealthy habit can be reframed. By that time, the patient should be feeling more powerful and confident about himself, as well as about your competence, and the chances of success with work on the second habit are increased. As we mentioned earlier, we have had many patients "spontaneously" change or discard other bad habits as a result of their initially reframing an identified unhealthy habit. Our assumption in these cases is that the patient has *unconsciously* reframed other bad habits. This can occur during the initial reframing (in which case, the patient would report on follow-up that he is pleasantly surprised that he has worked on Y as well as X), or this can occur later. The health professional can increase the probability of a patient's reframing other bad habits by suggesting that this possibility exists.

One caution: Don't be surprised if, on follow-up, a patient reports significant change in habit Y even if X had been focused upon during reframing. This will not be a rare occurrence. Our hypothesis in such cases is that the patient, in order to resist the health professional, has unconsciously reframed the other habit. In order to utilize such polarity responses we recommend that with particularly resistant patients who present with two unhealthy habits, the health professional insist on first reframing that habit *not* selected by the patient as a priority. This will often result in a "resistant" response of successful work on the more personal pressing habit.

ESTABLISHING COMMUNICATION WITH THE RESPONSIBLE UNCONSCIOUS "PART"

At first, this step of reframing sounds rather mysterious or magical. However, the concept that there is some inner or unconscious part responsible for a destructive habit fits the experience of most patients and is usually readily accepted by them. For example, patients will often report that even though they've wanted to give up an unhealthy habit, "something" prevented them from doing so. Many patients say, "It's an unconscious part of me that's responsible," or "It's not my fault; it's my unconscious." Instead of fighting with such patients and demanding that they take more responsibility for themselves, we prefer to utilize their energies positively.

Asking the patient to communicate with the unconscious part responsible for a habit also serves several other very useful purposes. For most patients who come to a clinical hypnotist,

X "What's your "phone no.?"
" What part of your s-conc mind does
that no. come from"? — It's always the same part

communicating with the unconscious paces their expectations that something different will take place. Furthermore, if experience related to an unhealthy habit is made more conscious, this heightened awareness in and of itself will often give the patient more control. Finally, the patient's experience of the unconscious part can often provide some important clinical data that can be utilized to help the patient (see the case study of R. M. at the end of this chapter).

A sophisticated modification of the second step of reframing can occur after the patient has become aware of the part responsible for the habit. At that point, the clinical hypnotist can request this part to provide "yes" and "no" signals for the patient, which will provide feedback to the patient and hypnotist during the trance. For example, these signals can be utilized to ascertain the accuracy of suggested payoffs of the habit or to signal whether alternatives to the habit are acceptable. Sometimes the therapist can simply suggest that the signal safely increase in intensity for "yes" or decrease in intensity for "no." The hypnotist can use his own creativity to help establish these signals. For example, if the patient has experienced the previously unconscious part as an image of a face, the clinical hypnotist can suggest that the face smile or nod up and down for "yes" or frown or shake back and forth for "no."

Another modification of this second step of reframing is to completely bypass the patient's consciousness and to ask that the unconscious part of the patient that's been responsible for the unhealthy habit communicate with *you*, the therapist. In such cases, *ideomotor signaling* by the patient would be employed. For example, the hypnotist can establish unconscious "yes" and "no" signals, such as suggesting that one of the patient's fingers spontaneously and slowly lift for "yes" and another finger lift for "no." Some therapists might prefer to use ideomotor signaling during reframing in order to prevent the possibility of any conscious contamination or manipulation by the patient.

We have found that it is not always necessary for the patient to be aware of the unconscious part responsible for the habit or for signals from that part to be established with the patient or with you. Some patients will report no such conscious aware-ness during trance, and sometimes ideomotor signaling will not be established. In such cases, it is suggested that the therapist simply go ahead with reframing by proceeding to the next step. On occasion, when we have purposely bypassed this step of re-framing entirely (for example, in cases when we did not feel this procedure would pace a particular patient), we have still been successful. In such cases, we still assume that we are being heard by this unconscious part of the patient, so we continue to communicate our respect and ask that it accept our commu-nication to it.

SUGGESTING THAT THE UNHEALTHY HABIT HAS HAD PAYOFFS

Realizing that an unhealthy habit has benefited the patient reframes the entire situation for the patient and the clinician. No longer is the clinician locked in combat with the patient, or more precisely, with the patient's resistance. Instead, the clin-ician and patient can proceed with the mutual understanding that the habitual disorder has helped out the patient and de-serves respect.

During this step of the reframing process we suggest that payoffs or benefits are involved. Since we have found that fur-ther work proceeds more smoothly if the concept of payoffs for a habit is accepted first by the patient, we do not proceed to the next step until we are sure the patient accepts this notion. We will often simply ask the patient in trance to nod his head if he or she accepts this idea.

Most persons accept this concept readily. However, some pa-tients may be confused and the therapist may find it necessary to rephrase his communication. In some cases, it may be neces-sary to ask the patient if she is willing to accept the notion of payoffs "for the time being" or if she is willing to "pretend" or to "imagine" that payoffs are involved before proceeding to ex-plore exactly what those payoffs are.

Some patients may have difficulty identifying the payoffs from an unhealthy habit. In such cases, the therapist can help

out by presenting a "multiple choice" array of possible payoffs
for the patient's consideration. Observing the patient's nonverbal reactions at such times can be particularly helpful in correctly identifying relevant payoffs. The case study of N. S. at the
end of this chapter illustrates the use of this multiple choice
communication strategy in the payoff step of reframing.

Payoffs for a destructive habit can be as unique and diversi-
fied as people themselves are. However, just as there are com-
monalities among people, we have found that there are some
common payoffs for habits. This is why knowledge of the particular disorder being treated is critically important. Some common payoffs are listed in Table 1. Two particularly prevalent
payoffs that bear mentioning here are stress management and
passive-aggressiveness or stubbornness.

TABLE 1
Some Common Payoffs From Habit Disorders

Cigarettes	Overeating/ Overweight	Alcoholism
stress management/ self tranquili- zation	stress management/ self tranquili- zation	stress management/ self tranquili- zation
stubborn/ independence	gratification/gift	gratification/gift
gratification/gift	stubborn/ independence	reliable "friend"/ "companion"
reliable "friend"/ "companion"	reliable "friend"/ "companion"	avoidance of intimate relationships
to model loved one(s)	avoidance of intimate relationships	excuse for acting out or irresponsible behavior
to eat less and avoid being overweight	avoidance of sexuality (one's own sexual im- pulses or im- pulses of others)	to fit in with the group
to stimulate (nicotine effect)	to model loved one(s)	relief of boredom
to breathe deeply	relief of boredom	to model loved one(s)
to socialize/fit in with the group	to socialize/fit in with the group	

Stress Management

For a variety of factors related to history, heredity or both, many persons become habituated to eating, smoking or drinking as a way to relieve stress or tension. Identifying the particular type or source of stress that the patient experiences and specifically how the unhealthy habit helps out enables the therapist to help the patient generate suitable alternatives. For example, for one of our overweight patients stress was a feeling of loneliness, and food helped her to feel better because it was associated in the patient's mind with people (and the patient often used meals to be with people). That patient joined a service club and a sorority to socialize more. For another patient, a source of stress was anxiety over "losing control" and looking foolish if he got angry. That patient became aware that a cigarette gave him a chance to take a break and regain his composure when his situation became stressful. Smoking a cigarette literally and symbolically helped him to "keep his mouth shut." As alternatives, the patient learned he didn't need a cigarette to take a break and that he could express himself more freely than he had thought possible without negative consequences. An alcoholic business executive used alcohol to calm down whenever he felt harried due to job pressures. He discovered that self-hypnosis was a healthier and more satisfying alternative.

Because an unhealthy habit so often serves the purpose of stress management, part of our normal screening procedure is to inquire whether a prospective patient is experiencing *extraordinary stress*, and we will usually not accept such cases. (Our screening recommendations are elaborated upon in Chapter 8.) Instead, we will recommend that the person wait until the level of stress has diminished or that he seek counseling. Because significant stress is so common after life crises or changes (e.g., separation or divorce, death of a loved one, a job change), a waiting period to allow a normal adjustment after such events is often helpful before treatment for an unhealthy habit is begun. We will, however, accept patients in such adjustment periods if the unhealthy habit is immediately life-threatening for the patient (e.g., a smoker with severe emphysema or an obese patient

with significant cardiovascular disease). Such high-risk patients
are usually highly motivated.

Passive Aggressiveness/Stubbornness

When you want to give up an unhealthy habit, it's often more
difficult to do so if someone else tells you, "You'd better stop."
No one likes to "give in." Virtually all patients with unhealthy
habits experience such conflicts. Mass media campaigns (e.g.,
the American Cancer Society's campaign against smoking cigarettes) are one thing. But when there is pressure from loved ones
or friends to stop smoking, to diet, or to stop drinking, the patient often "digs in" stubbornly as part of the power dynamics
present in all interpersonal relationships. For many persons, the
important payoff of an unhealthy habit is a passive expression
of aggression against a "persecutor" toward whom they otherwise feel powerless. The other person's complaints only serve
to fuel the fire by increasing the payoffs of engaging in the
habit.

Because such dynamics are common, part of our screening
procedure is to inquire whether the patient is being "bugged"
or "hounded" by anyone to give up the habit or if anyone is "on
the patient's back about it." Although this is often the case, we
will still accept most patients for treatment if there is some evidence of *patient* motivation to stop the unhealthy habit. However, if there are signs that the patient seeks treatment primarily "to make someone else happy," we will usually turn him down.

SUGGESTING THAT THE PATIENT
GENERATE ALTERNATIVE PATTERNS

This step of reframing relies on our firm belief that there are
always alternative realities, that is, other ways to see, hear, feel
or behave in the world. Within the reframing procedure, we point
out that there are other patterns of behavior that can provide
our patients with whatever payoffs or benefits unhealthy habits
have given to them, and these new patterns would be healthier
and more satisfying. Furthermore, we believe that most persons

have available to them the necessary resources to construct these new patterns of behavior. These resources are available within the patient's unconscious mind, which (conceptually) has stored within it every bit of data that the patient has experienced — and that's a lot of information! Certainly, it is enough information to construct whatever healthier patterns of behavior are needed by the patient. It may be important to emphasize here that new patterns of behavior may include not only actual overt patterns of behavior (such as exercising instead of smoking cigarettes) but also new ways of experiencing or perceiving (e.g., the realization that a payoff relied upon for many years in the past isn't required anymore).

When you are suggesting to a patient that alternative patterns be constructed, be sure to emphasize that the new patterns will be *safer and healthier*. This will prevent the substitution of other negative or unhealthy habits for the one being treated. For example, a common concern for cigarette smokers, often because of past experience, is that they will overeat and gain weight if they stop smoking. However, such occurrences have been rare among our patients. In fact, as we mentioned earlier, many patients who stop smoking cigarettes will eat in even healthier ways because they feel powerful about not smoking anymore and they apply (unconsciously) the reframing process to their eating patterns.

Some patients may have difficulty constructing healthier alternative patterns of behavior. In such situations there are several different strategies that you can use:

1) Present a multiple choice array of possible alternatives for the patient's consideration. In such cases, it is particularly important to observe the patient's nonverbal cues or reactions in identifying suitable alternatives.
2) Direct the patient to work (consciously and unconsciously) on constructing alternatives between therapeutic sessions.
3) Suggest that the patient identify with someone else whom he likes or admires. Then the patient can construct alternatives that the identified person uses or would use to get needed payoffs.

4) As modification of this strategy related to number 2 above, direct the patient to observe, between therapeutic sessions, what patterns of behavior other persons employ to get similar payoffs.

Some patients require therapeutic support over time in order to experience or use alternative patterns. Expressing anger instead of swallowing it (and then tranquilizing oneself with food, cigarettes or alcohol) can be very terrifying for some patients. Asking for affection or needed intimacy through more and more honesty and openness (instead of gratifying oneself with excess food or buffering emotional pain with alcohol) can be equally frightening. Some patients may need support to explore various alternative patterns of behavior, and through trial and error over time find those that are most beneficial.

ECOLOGICALLY CHECKING NEW ALTERNATIVES

After the patient has constructed healthier alternatives that provide needed payoffs, it is helpful to "check out" these alternatives, especially with that part of the patient that was responsible for the unhealthy habit. Actually, such checks will often take place *while* the unconscious is generating the alternatives. As a result, some clinicians may choose, at times, to delete this step of reframing. However, when direct communication has been established with the unconscious part of the patient that was responsible for the unhealthy habit, we feel that it would be disrespectful to ignore that part of the person. The ecological check is carried out by asking this part of the person to communicate or to signal to the patient and to you if the new alternatives will be comfortable. Furthermore, all other parts of the person are asked to check out the alternatives for their suitability. We often ask the patient to take a few moments to be certain that the alternatives *seem*, *sound* and *feel* comfortable and suitable.* The ecological check is basically a check for congru-

*Visual, auditory and kinesthetic are the three primary representational systems for experiencing. The concept and utilization of the representational systems of experiencing are discussed more fully in Chapter 2.

ence – that is, do the alternative patterns of behavior fit in comfortably with all the important systems or with the total environment of the person?

As always, it is important to observe the nonverbal or unconscious behavior of the person when you are doing an ecological check of alternatives. We believe that the unconscious does not lie or distort as the conscious mind often does. Therefore, if the patient consciously reports that alternative patterns check out, but his nonverbal behavior (bodily tension or tightness or an ideomotor "no" signal) says something else, then there is obvious incongruence to be explored.

If there is evidence that alternative patterns do not check out, then the therapist should provide the patient with the opportunity to become aware of more suitable alternatives or to discover payoff(s) not identified.

FUTURE PACING

This final step of reframing involves asking the patient to imagine using the newly constructed patterns of behavior within relevant future contexts. These future situations are those which will be cue situations for needed payoffs. They are usually the same as or similar to past settings in which the unhealthy habit occurred. When future pacing, the therapist should suggest that the patient imagine future relevant situations, one by one, and in as much detail as possible, and to imagine using the healthier alternative patterns of behavior.

Future pacing serves two purposes: 1) a further and more complete check of the newly constructed alternative patterns of behavior, and 2) mental rehearsal for using the new alternatives, which tends to facilitate their use.

The clinical hypnotist can help with future pacing by reminding the patient of relevant settings that precipitated the unhealthy habit in the past. This process is enhanced by a thorough knowledge of common cue situations (e.g., talking on the phone, driving, or morning coffee for cigarette smokers; holiday parties for alcoholics), as well as particular settings or situations revealed during the intake interview with the patient.

During future pacing, we usually use a variation of the anchoring technique discussed in Chapter 3. First, we set up the anchor by establishing a relationship between a stimulus we can initiate, usually a touch on the shoulder, and an experience of feeling powerful. Then we instruct the patient to imagine herself at various times in the near future when *in the past* she would have engaged in the old habit. Now, however, the patient experiences herself engaging in one of the healthier alternatives that was generated during the reframing process. When the patient signals (and behaviorally designates) that she is engaging in this experience, a power anchor is fired. Thus, the patient is feeling powerful while imagining herself engaging in the new behavior, reinforcing the preceding reframing.

REFRAMING THROUGH THE USE OF METAPHORS AND STORIES

An interesting and elegant way to accomplish a reframing, which illustrates the Ericksonian use of indirect suggestions, is through the use of metaphors and storytelling (described in detail in Chapter 4). For example, here is the case of S. B., a 31-year-old single woman who was 5'2" tall and weighed 214 pounds. This patient stated that she was at a normal weight as a youngster but began quickly to put on weight around the age of 16; she had been obese from that time on. She revealed that just prior to putting on that weight she had been a victim of sexual assault, which both angered and frightened her. The therapist hypothesized that a significant payoff of S. B.'s obesity was to make her unattractive and thus protect her from sexual advances. Furthermore, her obesity helped S. B. to feel bigger and safer. While S. B. was in trance, the therapist told her the following reframing story instead of involving her in a six-step reframing. This strategic move was designed to avoid any possible discomfort that might result if her situation was dealt with more directly.

You know, the other day I ran into a friend of mine by the name of Susan and she told me something interesting. For many years, she has lived across the street from a beautiful woods and has regularly taken a walk along one particular path in those woods. As she walked along that path, Susan would look at the beauty of the woods, listen to the whistling of the birds, and feel the soft earth beneath her feet. The path led to a pretty clearing and she liked to rest there. She would feel comforted and strengthened at that spot. One day as she was walking from the clearing down her path, a small animal ran out of the bushes right across Susan's feet and nipped at her. It scared her and made her angry and she ran down the path, out of the woods and into her house. She locked the doors, pulled down the shades and stayed there for a while until she had to come out to go to work and to take care of her responsibilities. The only way Susan could feel comfortable going outside was to wear many layers of clothes over her entire body. She wore several shirts and sweaters and a heavy thick coat, even though it was warm outside. She wore several pairs of pants, gloves, boots and even a hat. She went around like that for quite a while, looking ridiculous and feeling weighted down and uncomfortable because of all the clothes. But at least Susan felt safe.

One day, as she was passing by her old path in the woods and looking longingly at the woods, wishing that she could walk through the woods again, she ran into a very wise old neighbor who asked her what was going on. Susan explained what had happened that day with the animal, how afraid it made her and how she could only feel comfortable wearing the layers of clothes.

The neighbor said, "Listen, there are all kinds of animals in the woods, some safe, some dangerous. I want to advise you to use the knowledge that you already have and to gain more knowledge if you need to, to know what to look for, what to listen for, what

to sense and feel so that you can tell the difference
between an animal that is safe and one that is dangerous. Learn how you can protect yourself if you
ever need to. For example, you can just yell real loud
and stomp your feet, and many animals will just turn
and run away. Learn whatever you need to learn. And
then, take the risk to come outside with one less layer
of clothing. Walk around like that and as you feel safe
and comfortable doing so, take off something else that
you don't need to wear. I want to advise you also to
take another path in the woods, because the woods
have many paths. Walk down that path, and if it feels
comfortable and if it is beautiful enough, keep on going. If not, turn around and take another path and
go further and further down the path that you choose
as long as it feels comfortable and safe enough. And,
as you feel safe and comfortable doing so, take off a
layer of clothing now and then that is unnecessary
and go further and further into the woods. Go on until
you find a path that will take you to a clearing—because many paths lead to a clearing—that will comfort you and strengthen you." And the wise old neighbor leaned down and whispered a secret into Susan's
ear, a very wise secret.*

Susan left, remembering what she had heard, and
came outside the next day wearing one less sweater.
Soon she took a path, didn't like it and so she found
another one and went further and further into the
woods, taking off a layer of unnecessary clothing only
as she felt safe and comfortable doing so. At the same
time, she read more and more about animals, learning
which were safe and which were dangerous and what
to do if she ever needed to protect herself from a dangerous animal. Eventually, she was walking down a

---

*This communication about a wise secret sets into motion the patient's uncon-
scious resources and potentials for healthy changes and is discussed more fully
in Chapter 4.

beautiful path wearing only the clothes that she needed to wear depending upon the conditions. That path
took her to a beautiful clearing which comforted her
and strengthened her and things have really gone well
for her.

At the next treatment session several weeks later, S. B. had
lost 11 pounds. At that session she expressed an interest in
wanting to work on sensitive issues that she believed were related to her sexual assault. In the months that followed, S. B.
lost over 70 pounds.

In another case, a patient became aware that an important
payoff for his smoking cigarettes was stubbornness: He didn't
want to give in to the persistent requests of family members
that he quit. To him, smoking symbolized his independence and
integrity. The following story was told to him during a six-step
reframing:

You know, Jim, what we're dealing with here reminds me of something that happened to me. Back in
1971 I had finished all the course work and all the exams that I needed to complete to get a Ph.D. I started working full-time, knowing that I had the evenings
and weekends to work on my research. It was a challenge, but certainly something that I knew I could do.
Once every couple of months I would go home to visit
my parents. I remember that as soon as I walked in
the house my mother would ask me about my dissertation. She'd say, "Charlie, how's it coming with that
work?" And I remember feeling irritated. Another
time I came home and my mom said, "How's the research coming?" And I felt real bugged by that. I
came home another time and my mother asked me
about it again and said, "You know, you're not going
to get anywhere until you get that done." And I remember that I wasn't getting it done. I just felt stuck.
Quite a long time went by, a few years as a matter
of fact. It was the spring of 1973 and I decided that

I really wanted to do something about it. I always felt kind of uncomfortable knowing I should be working on that dissertation. It was a burden, and I felt kind of guilty about it. I decided to spend an afternoon dealing with the problem and I went into my trance and I became aware of a part of me that felt real angry. Another part of me asked, "Well, what are you angry about?" And my answer was "because people are bugging me." And I remember saying, "I want to be independent. I don't want to give into other people or their demands." And then a part of me said, "Well you can be independent, but how independent are you really being if you're reacting so much to the demands of your mother? If you want to do your dissertation, then do it for yourself and feel good about that."

Then I became aware of another part of me that felt scared and I asked that part of me, "Well, what are you afraid of?" And my answer was that I was afraid of being a *doctor* and I was afraid of whatever responsibilities that would mean. I was afraid that I wouldn't be able to be "happy-go-lucky Charlie" anymore. And I said to that part of me, "Listen, getting that dissertation done and being a doctor will open up doors for you but it's always your choice to go through them or not. You can be a doctor and that will be helpful. You can be happy-go-lucky Charlie when you need or want to be that." I remember that I felt much more comfortable and I got that dissertation done soon after.

CASE STUDIES

N. S. (Weight Loss)

N. S. was a 31-year-old woman married for 10 years; she had no children. She worked as a school teacher; her husband was employed as an electrical engineer. She described her marriage as having its "ups and downs." She was 5'4" tall, weighed 160 pounds, and desired to diet and lose 35 pounds. When she got married, N. S. weighed 125 pounds, but she gained weight steadily and for the last five or six years had fluctuated between 150 and 165 pounds. She had tried various diets with little success. She reported that her husband often mentioned to her that she was overweight and this irritated her. However, she also seemed quite motivated herself to diet.

During reframing N. S. experienced that part of her that was responsible for her overeating and being overweight as a "tight, scary feeling in my stomach," but she was unable to say what she felt scared about. After accepting the concept that overeating or being overweight had payoffs or benefited her, she was unable to identify what the payoffs were. In order to help her out, the therapist then presented a multiple choice array of possible payoffs as follows:

> "Now I don't really know what payoffs you've gotten by overeating and being overweight, but I can recall what some other patients have become aware of. One woman who was here the day before yesterday became aware that for her eating was a way to comfort and gratify herself when she felt lonely, which occurred often in her case. Another lady who was in a troubled marriage became aware that she was afraid to lose weight because it was the first step in her possibly leaving the marriage to find a more suitable mate and she wanted to avoid the hurt of a separation and divorce. She also was afraid to be alone if she did separate from her husband. (*N. S. tightened up noticeably and got teary-eyed when this was mentioned.*) A man who was here several weeks ago became aware that food was a solution to his often felt boredom. A young woman who was here a month ago discovered that she couldn't diet because she was angry and resentful at the demands of her father that she lose weight. (*N. S. grimaced when she heard this.*)

After mentioning a few more possible payoffs, the clinician gently focused on the two payoff areas that N. S. had reacted to and the patient became aware of the relevance of these payoffs to her situation. With the clinician's support, N. S. explored healthier alternatives to overeating and being overweight that would provide her with the safety she needed but be more satisfying. She decided to risk beginning to lose weight with the realization that this might "open up doors for her" but that it was always her choice to go through them or not.

After this session, N. S. began to be more assertive and honest with her husband instead of passively resisting him by not giving in to his demands to lose weight. These alternative patterns helped N. S. to feel more powerful and to deal more constructively with the problems in her marriage. As of this writing, she and her husband are in marriage counseling and she has met her goal of losing 35 pounds.

R. M. (Cigarette Smoking)

R. M. was a 44-year-old married male who had been smoking cigarettes since he was 16. He was in a stable marriage, had two children, 11 and 14, and was a partner in a stock brokerage firm. R. M. had stopped smoking cigarettes a half a dozen times, but never longer than several days. He stated that he wanted to stop because of health concerns but felt he needed help to do so. His wife did not smoke and was supportive of his efforts. R. M. was a light drinker of alcohol and was in good health. R. M.'s parents were deceased; both died in their fifties from smoking-related disorders.

During reframing, when R. M. was asked to become aware of that part of his unconscious responsible for smoking, he felt a warm, comfortable feeling as he remembered riding in the back seat of his parents' car when he was a young boy. He remembered the smell of cigarette smoke drifting lazily to the back of the car. The patient's parents often took him for long rides in the country and the memory was a very pleasant one.

As the reframing continued, R. M. became aware that the main payoffs from smoking cigarettes were: 1) to calm down when he felt tense or upset, and 2) to access a warm, comfortable feeling associated with his parents that cigarettes triggered within him. As alternatives to smoking, R. M. decided to use deep breathing and self-hypnosis to help him when he felt tense, and to spend time regularly experiencing positive feelings and memories associated with his parents.

However, during the "ecological check" part of reframing, R. M. experienced some tension. When that was explored, he became aware that he felt guilty about the prospect of not smoking anymore and of quite possibly living much longer than his beloved parents. At this point, R. M. felt comfortable accepting the therapist's suggestion to imagine seeing his parents in his own mind, to talk with them about his guilt and to get their "permission" to stop smoking and to live as long as he could. After this, R. M. was able to feel comfortable and he hasn't smoked in over two years.

This case illustrates the importance of obtaining data on family members of the patient who may have modeled unhealthy habits. It is often necessary to defuse the power of such modeling with clinical strategies similar to those employed with R. M.

H. L. (Alcoholism)

H. L., 45, was a foreman for a printing company. He was on probation for a drunk driving charge and in jeopardy of losing his job because of absenteeism and lateness. When he called for an appointment he admitted that he had been drinking for several days. He was depressed and asked for help. H. L. was admitted to a local hospital for alcohol detoxification. He was advised that he should inform his employer that he was seeking help. When he did so, he was granted "one last chance" to return to his job when physically able to do so. He was seen for clinical hypnotic treatment on the first day he was discharged from the hospital.

H. L. reported feeling depressed and scared when asked to experience the part responsible for his excessive drinking. As the reframing continued, these payoffs for drinking were identified: 1) alcohol buffered his depression (specifically, a good deal

of hurt and anger associated with his divorce, as well as anxiety and tension due to pressure from supervisors at work for
better performance). 2) When drinking, H. L. was outgoing and
enthusiastic in social situations, which was very reinforcing for
him. He enjoyed socializing in bars and with his "drinking bud-
dies." However, he was basically a shy and quiet person.

H. L. generated the following alternatives for the payoffs that
drinking had given to him. First, he joined Alcoholics Anonymous and began attending meetings three or four nights weekly.
The friendly and accepting atmosphere there helped H. L. feel
comfortable and his needs to socialize with others began to be
met. H. L. also entered into psychotherapy and resolved many
of the issues left over from his divorce. Then he learned to be
accepting of his reserved nature but to be assertive when necessary. Finally, as is often true in such cases, H. L. found that his
work problems, as well as many other problems, cleared up when
he maintained sobriety and when he looked into his emotional
difficulties.

In the case of H. L., the reframing process took a number of
hours over the course of several hypnotherapeutic sessions. H.
L. had agreed to maintain sobriety during treatment and his sobriety continued after termination from treatment. He has continued to be active in A. A. and at this writing has maintained
sobriety for three years.

Reframing—helping a patient to see his or her world more
positively and to use healthier patterns of behavior—is an integral part of most psychotherapeutic pursuits. Certainly any
therapist treating habit disorders should be well versed in the
strategies necessary to accomplish this.

CHAPTER 7

MEDICAL ASPECTS OF HABIT DISORDERS

AS A CLINICIAN seeking to work with habit disorders, what are *your* beliefs about these disorders?

When is alcohol use a problem?

How should a physician be involved in the treatment of drug-dependent conditions?

At what point is it appropriate to refer an overweight patient for a metabolic and/or endocrinological evaluation?

Here we present our beliefs in approaching patients with these problems, in counterpoint to some standard positions (which the curious reader might wish to consult in greater detail for his or her own interest).

SOME DEFINITIONS

We will start out with some recent definitions from Frederick Hofmann's *A Handbook on Drug and Alcohol Abuse: The Biomedical Aspects* (1983):

1. Physical Dependence: When certain drugs are taken on a regular schedule in appropriate quantities, the state known as physical dependence develops. The drugs known to produce physical dependence are the

narcotics and the generalized central nervous system depressants, which include such sedative and hypnotic tranquilizers as meprobamate (Miltown) (p. 55).

Physical dependence upon drugs is occult in that, as long as drug intake remains adequate, its existence can in no way be detected either by the addict or by an observer. The presence of physical dependence can be determined only if the intake of drug is stopped abruptly or markedly reduced, for then an involuntary physiological illness develops. This is called the withdrawal or abstinence syndrome (p. 56).

2. Psychological Dependence: The only condition common to all forms of chronic drug abuse is psychological or psychic dependence, which are synonymous terms used to describe the user's attitude toward the taking of drugs and the effects they produce. This attitude is such that "the effects produced by a drug, or the conditions associated with its use, are necessary to maintain an optimal state of well being" (p. 52).

The degree or intensity of psychological dependence present in an individual user cannot be measured precisely and is usually described by such words as mild, moderate, or marked. Most users of addicting drugs eventually develop marked psychological dependence, whereas such dependence may vary from extremely mild to marked among users of non-addicting drugs. With drug addiction, the compulsive use (see below) of drugs may stem, in part, from fear of the withdrawal syndrome (p. 53).

In the standard medical pharmacology text, *Goodman and Gilman's The Pharmacological Basis of Therapeutics* (1980), Jerome Jaffe discusses the concepts of compulsive drug use and addiction. He defines *compulsive drug use* as a pattern of dependence on a drug that alters mood or that is "characterized by diminished flexibility in terms of behavior toward a particular drug." The drug is taken despite the absence of medical indication. It should be clearly noted that there is no reference in this description to a physiological basis for this belief. It is significant that an important part of this definition is that the use of the drug in question is considered to be detrimental to the user or to society. For example, cigarette smoking has undergone a change from a relatively unquestioned habit to one that is reviled as medical evidence over the last 10 to 15 years has heightened societal awareness of the dangers of smoking. The permissive attitude has disappeared as the evidence of the deleterious effects of tobacco smoke in relation to pulmonary and cardiovascular diseases has become indisputable.

Jaffe defines addiction as further down the continuum of compulsive drug use in that it is drug use that is more pervasive in the person's life. Addiction is a behavior pattern of drug use characterized by overwhelming involvement with the use of a drug and the securing of its supply, as well as a high tendency to relapse after withdrawal. Jaffe's definitions of compulsive drug use and addiction cannot be used interchangeably with physical dependence. In both cases, he stresses the psychological component (Jaffe, 1980).

Another important term is *tolerance*, which is frequently confused with physical dependence. Tolerance generally occurs with those drugs which cause physical dependence, although it is not restricted to these drugs. Tolerance describes the decrease in intensity of effect that occurs as a substance is given repeatedly over time—as the body adapts to it. In order to get the same effect, the size of the dose must be increased or administration of the drug must be discontinued until tolerance abates (Hofmann, 1983, p. 60).

The complex relationship between the physical and psychological is reflected in data from some interesting experiments regarding conditioning as reinforcement. If administration of morphine to a rat is repeatedly paired with the ringing of a bell, classical conditioning occurs; the animal will then display physiological indications of the presence of the drug with the ringing of the bell only. Furthermore, administration of a narcotic antagonist in these cases will precipitate withdrawal.

Jaffe comments:

Such conditioning helps to explain how the rituals
and circumstances surrounding drug use can act as
secondary reinforcers, and how the mere taking of an
inert pill or the use of a needle and syringe containing
no drug can evoke the feelings (including relief of
withdrawal symptoms) previously produced when the
pill or syringe contained an active substance. The
observation that withdrawal distress can become con-
ditioned to the environment in which it occurs may
underlie reports that former opioid addicts may experience sensations very similar to withdrawal symptoms, including an intensified craving for drugs,
when they return to an environment where drugs are
available. Alcoholics may have similar experiences,
particularly when they are exposed to the sight and
smell of alcohol. . . . The conditions that elicit the most
severe withdrawal and the most intense "craving" for
opioids are those associated with the availability and
use of the drug, rather than those associated with
withdrawal (Jaffe, 1980, p. 543).

Social factors play a major role in habit disorders. People
drink with friends, smoke together, eat, or talk about eating
together. Even when people pursue their destructive habits in
a solitary fashion, there are interpersonal aspects to their behavior. For instance, a person might gorge himself with food
because he is alone, or go on an alcoholic binge when he has been
disappointed by a loved one.

The social aspects of habit disorders may be seen clearly
when we consider smoking as an example. We frequently learn
that most people begin to smoke as teenagers, as a way of asserting their independence and identifying with the peer group.
The positive effect of belonging to the "gang" explains in part
why first-time smokers persist in the habit despite extremely
unpleasant initial experiences – nicotine frequently causes nausea the first few times it is used.

For example, we are unaware of any food which causes physical dependence in the precise sense defined earlier. Yet, if a per-

son says that he would suffer withdrawal symptoms upon the cessation of sweets and on further questioning we learn that he is speaking literally and not metaphorically, we will describe our interventions as being particularly useful in dealing with "just such dependencies." We strongly advise you to resist the temptation to pull down your trusty reference work, which states unequivocally that sweets (or whatever) "have never been proven to cause physical dependence when subjected to a well-designed double-bind crossover research study." Rather, utilize your patient's statement as a gift.

One patient, Jan, was struggling with her weight. She would diet excessively for about ten days and then gorge herself on sweets, wiping out the weight loss. During the initial data-gathering, she spoke of her strong addiction to sweets. Consequently, she was told the following:

> I am glad that you realize that your problem has a physiological basis. Clearly you can see why severe dietary restrictions have not been effective: When you remove the sweets from your diet, your body reacts very violently and you have to gorge yourself to re-establish physical well-being. It is clear to me that you sincerely wish to lose weight, and therefore, I know that it will be a lot easier for you to understand that the rapid weight loss you achieved was unhealthy for you because it was at the expense of your physical well-being. Consequently, you will need to continue to eat sweets in the manner which we will discuss so as to be able to wean yourself from them. Obviously, your weight loss will be slow, no more than two pounds a week for the first two weeks. In fact, that may be too much.

Note that this communication, along with the prescription to eat sweets that would then follow, is an example of a symptom prescription, which in and of itself can promote substantial change, even without trance work. For a full description of this matter, see Chapter 5.

THE BOTTOM LINE: PATIENTS DON'T
READ PHARMACOLOGY TEXTS

In clinical practice, the fine distinctions made in the definitions discussed above (which in the scientific community tend to be presented as truths) are likely to be largely irrelevant, since they may not reflect the beliefs and understandings of your patients (unless, of course, they *do* read pharmacology books). Indeed, the only way to know what your patients believe is to listen to them.

Clinical effectiveness increases dramatically when therapists solicit their patients' beliefs and understandings and initially accept them, rather than arguing with them or telling them that they don't "really" understand the way things are. Once the beliefs of patients are paced, they can be led to other beliefs that will be more helpful.

Paul Watzlawick has pointed out that most therapists, rather than learning the patient's language, try to teach the patient the new language of therapy (be it psychoanalytic, existential, Gestalt, transactional analysis, etc.), and then require the patient to translate her everyday behavior (for which she has her own very satisfactory, although perhaps idiosyncratic, language) into the therapists' terms. We recall that one of the hallmarks of Erickson's work was his ability to speak the language of the person he was treating.

The importance of beliefs is also demonstrated by the fact that, despite the sound scientific evidence for physical dependence on nicotine (Goodman et al., 1980), many smokers become non-smokers "cold turkey," without any symptoms of withdrawal. It therefore behooves the clinician to ascertain the beliefs of the patient.

SOME REMARKS ABOUT ALCOHOL,
NICOTINE, AND FOOD

Alcohol

Alcohol is classified pharmacologically as a central nervous system depressant. For some individuals a single small dose (two to four ounces of whiskey) appears to have the effect of improving performance on intellectual tasks. It is unclear, however, whether this effect results from direct stimulation of the central nervous system or from release of some emotional controls. The problem drinker, however, demonstrates the physiological effects of moderate to marked drug ingestion. The following behaviors are seen with moderate alcohol ingestion:

> Ordinary restraints on speech and behavior are weakened ("release of inhibitions"), euphoria may develop, self-confidence is often increased, and there are reductions in neuromuscular coordination (manifested in speech, gait, and manual dexterity), visual acuity, and perception of pain and fatigue. In addition, reaction time is prolonged, memory, insight, and the ability to concentrate are impaired . . . (Hofmann, 1983, p. 101).

There is a great deal of variability among individuals regarding the amount ingested before such behaviors are manifested:

> At low blood alcohol concentrations (50 mg/100 ml or less), 10% of a population of drinkers appear intoxicated (as determined by trained observers utilizing such criteria as slurred speech, obvious loss of inhibitions, and locomotor difficulties). At levels regarded as significant both medically and legally (for example, 101 to 150 mg/100 ml), just 64% appear intoxicated. Only at levels exceeding 200 mg/100 ml do virtually all drinkers appear intoxicated (Hofmann, 1983, p. 102).

Chronic alcohol ingestion leads to tolerance of the central nervous system manifestations, such that an alcoholic with a blood concentration "as high as 300 mg/100 ml may appear only mildly intoxicated" (Hofmann, 1983, p. 102). Experimental evidence shows that there is great individual variation in alcohol tolerance and that there is no way to predict how someone will metabolize and, more importantly, manifest a given dose of the substance.

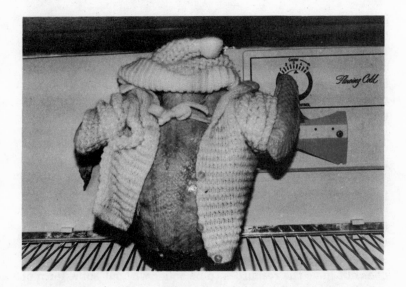

The alcohol withdrawal syndrome can occur after a few hours of moderate intoxication (the "hangover"). Another withdrawal manifestation following several days of continuous marked intoxication is tremulousness. The most traumatic manifestation of abstinence, "psychotic delirium, occurred . . . only after 400 to 500 ml of alcohol/day had been consumed for 48 or more days. . . . It may nevertheless be said that both the nature and intensity of the alcohol withdrawal syndrome appear to depend usually on the degree and duration of chronic intoxication before abstinence or a sharp reduction in intake" (Hofmann, 1983, p. 110).

The interested reader is referred to the standard texts for complete details of the other harmful effects of alcohol to organ systems and for description of chronic medical conditions secondary to prolonged intoxication (such as peripheral neuropathy, amblyoopia, Wernicke's encephalopathy) (see, for example, Hofmann, 1983, p. 113 ff).

Every patient referred for hypnotherapeutic treatment of alcohol abuse should have a complete medical evaluation. Should the patient be found to be chronically intoxicated, he or she must be detoxified, usually on an inpatient basis, before hypnotic treatment begins. There is evidence that in a supportive inpatient environment most alcoholic patients can undergo detoxification without pharmacological support (Whitfield et al., 1978). Frequently, a problem drinker will not need detoxification despite intermittent, though marked, episodes of acute intoxication. In either case, it is helpful for the individual to get an assessment of the physical effects, if any, of his alcohol use. This may serve to increase motivation (should any abnormalities be found during the medical examination). On the other hand, the marginally motivated individual, pushed in by family members, may opt out of treatment when detoxification and a medical evaluation are required. This saves the clinician much valuable time and energy.

Let us say a word about Antabuse. This drug, when taken faithfully, causes an individual to have a violent reaction to a very small amount of ingested alcohol. In general, we prefer to avoid this form of treatment, since it indicates that the patient does not have the resources to be sober without some form of drug, and this undercuts the basic philosophy of our approach. Furthermore, we generally avoid aversive treatments, and the nausea which these people experience using this drug is severe. In addition, use of this medication requires close coordination with the prescribing individual, and signals can be crossed, leading to a significant compromise of the hypnotherapist's flexibility. However, on occasion we have treated alcoholic patients taking Antabuse: one treatment objective in such cases is to help the patient take the medication regularly until it is decided that the Antabuse regimen be terminated, at which time sobriety without Antabuse would be maintained.

The concept of alcoholism as a disease is widely accepted by both professionals and the general community. There is, however, a well-articulated alternative perspective that alcoholic behavior is essentially a social phenomenon. In their prize-winning sociological study, *Deviance and Medicalization: From Badness to Sickness* (1980), Conrad and Schneider describe the trend in our society to medicalize deviant behavior. They note that the disease called "alcoholism" in many ways does not satisfy strict medical criteria. This "disease" is described not in terms of its physiological effects, but rather by its interference with social functioning. Indeed, most alcoholics do not seem to be physically dependent; i.e., they do not suffer withdrawal symptoms following cessation of drinking. Conrad and Schneider do not deny the significance of alcohol use in our society. They simply point out the fact that there are some glaring inconsistencies in our definition of alcoholism as a disease. They trace the fact that the medicalization of this aberrant behavior was an attempt to deal with an important problem, but they say that the use of the medical model may be quite inappropriate if the use and abuse of alcohol is not a disease (Conrad and Schneider, 1980).

Nicotine

Physiologically, nicotine has central nervous system stimulant properties. It also causes muscle relaxation, facilitates memory, and decreases appetite and irritability. Nicotine reaches the brain within eight seconds after inhalation of smoke. Tolerance develops to some of nicotine's effects, but the cardiovascular effects (increased blood pressure and pulse rate) still occur in chronic smokers after one or two cigarettes. These effects are greater following the first cigarette of the day (Gilman et al., 1980).

The appearance of a withdrawal syndrome following cessation of cigarette smoking is quite variable. There appears to be "virtually no information on what levels of exposure are required to induce physical dependence in man." The signs and symptoms attributed to withdrawal include "nausea, headache, constipation, diarrhea, and increased appetite. Drowsiness, fatigue, sleep disturbances (insomnia), irritability (increased hostility), and inability to concentrate are also common" (Gilman et al., 1980, p. 559). The pharmacology texts go on and on, and a grave error can be made by memorizing this list and presenting it to your patients: The power of the clinician's words can lead to disastrous results, as the "responsible sharing of information" turns into a self-fulfilling prophecy.

There are a few facts which are useful, however. It seems that abruptly stopping cigarettes may make more sense than tapering off, which may merely prolong the period of discomfort. Some heavy smokers adjust their patterns of smoking to keep the amount of nicotine they inhale constant; if a cigarette has higher nicotine, they reduce the number smoked and change the intensity of their puffing. For these people, it may follow that changing to a low-nicotine brand will only serve to increase the number of cigarettes smoked. The literature states that of the individuals who seek some kind of help to stop smoking, only 20-40% are abstinent after one year (Gilman et al., 1980). The data that we have collected show a success rate of around 80% abstinence for the first four months following treatment. This reflects not only the soundness of our techniques (especially Reframing, Chapter 6), but also the stringent screening we use for accepting patients for treatment (Chapter 8).

Nicorette gum, which has recently been released on the American market, deserves special mention. This prescription medication contains nicotine in a resin complex. Since it is our preference to follow the cues from our patients, we do not discuss this medication unless they speak about grave concerns regarding withdrawal, either on the basis of previous failures to quit or in response to questions about the use of the substance. In such a case, we would ask them whether they felt that they were addicted and needed this support, and we would respond in a way congruent with their beliefs.

Food

Many overweight patients secretly harbor the desire that their problem be related to a physical condition ("glandular or hormonal problem"), since then they would be off the hook as far as taking responsibility for being fat. The hypnotherapist increases his or her effectiveness by assessing the strength of the patient's beliefs in this area and making a referral for a medical evaluation if one has not occurred recently. We believe that a patient who still holds out for the possibility of a medical cause may not be sufficiently motivated to apply the necessary energy to his or her part of the active intervention required to change the old patterns of behavior.

Some knowledge of nutrition is a prerequisite for restructuring poor eating habits. It is fair to say that most people who come for weight management have used many diets in the past. However, many of these may well have been fad diets which, while generally quite successful in promoting rapid initial weight loss (and generous royalties from rapid book sales), are poor models for long-term dietary change. Many patients need to completely restructure the way they eat. The comprehensive diet plan offered by Weight Watchers is one example of a sound program for dietary management.

Since the word "diet" is used for nutritionally balanced plans such as Weight Watchers as well as for severe restrictive approaches such as the liquid protein diet, it is mandatory that the clinican be assured that the patient understands the guidelines of good nutrition. Briefly stated, this includes a mixture of protein, fat, and carbohydrates in the ratio of 2 : 3 : 5 (Goodheart and Shils, 1980). Most often, the best dietary strategy involves regularizing food intake throughout the day. Eating several small meals (not necessarily three) seems preferable to having one large meal in diminishing the tendency to grossly overeat at that single sitting. Eating only one meal is associated with the rationalization that the person is providing all her daily energy at that time. We believe that patients have a more difficult time modifying their eating patterns when they are ravenous after a long period of abstinence. One is reminded of the advice to avoid food shopping when hungry: "The eyes are much bigger than the stomach." Furthermore, when a person eats only once a day, that meal is likely to become the focus of attention and anticipation. Such obsessive focusing is probably detrimental to our goal of having eating become a more automatic, though not necessarily less pleasurable, part of the day. When someone eats on a regular, predictable basis, food may take on less heightened significance.

We strongly recommend that you avail yourself of the services of a skilled clinical nutritionist. This person can provide you with guidelines for proper nutrition, which will enable you to determine just how appropriate a patient's knowledge is. As you evaluate a patient's eating habits and knowledge of nutrition, you may learn that there are glaring gaps. A referral to the nutritionist is then in order.

Some patients may misrepresent their eating habits – either consciously, because they are ashamed of their bad habits, or unconsciously, because they believe that they "know" what a proper diet is. If this is the case, you will probably find that their weight loss is less than expected. Further investigation will provide the information necessary, and the nutritionist can aid the patient in being honest with himself and the therapist.

Dietary modification (reduction in fuel ingested) and increased energy expenditure (physical activity) are the two complementary processes which lead to a reduction in weight. Although we strongly recommend regular physical activity, we often avoid the word "exercise," which has such negative connotations for most overweight people. Many of us believe that we have to work up a good sweat in order to burn off those extra pounds. This is far from the truth. It is usually a pleasant surprise to many people to learn that walking a mile consumes the same amount of energy, and therefore leads to the same amount of weight loss, as running a mile. The only advantages of running are that it is more efficient time-wise and promotes cardiovascular fitness. The concept of "increased activity via lifestyle change" has become increasingly popular with overweight patients who balk at the idea of a program of vigorous exercise. Frequently, it is beneficial to encourage these reluctant individuals to utilize everyday situations in a healthy way – for example, walking up and down stairs instead of always using the elevator or parking the car a couple of blocks away from work and walking the remaining distance. Likewise, we recommend that they park their car at shopping malls at the far end of the parking lot and walk that distance to the entrance. Some of our patients accept these changes more readily than a regimen of athletic activity. As the changes become a part of their lives, they serve as healthful new patterns which can be accomplished automatically.

Most overweight individuals desire a method that will *rapidly* cause the fat to "melt away." (To measure the prevalence of such hopes just examine the current *National Enquirer* at your supermarket check-out.) This seems a bit magical to us, and we certainly don't expect this to occur following the start of hypnotherapy. However, most folks think of hypnosis as magic, and the clinician must be ever mindful of the patient's expectations. We frequently address this issue by telling the patient that she may well have rapidly lost weight in small amounts before, but that she probably would not be coming for treatment if that approach were successful. We say that our goal is to promote controlled, long-lasting weight loss, and that since the weight gain had occurred over a period of time, it would be unreasonable to expect the weight loss to occur in so short a time.

The clinician should be mindful of the stages that occur in weight loss produced by significant dietary restructuring. There is a significant weight loss at the beginning of a new diet plan, which involves mostly a loss of water. The patient who is initially elated by this fact may become quite disheartened when she reaches the plateau which frequently occurs, sometimes weeks, sometimes months, into treatment. Part of the plateau may relate to temporary water retention or other concomitant medical conditions. Also, the body's metabolism slows down as the amount of food intake decreases. We believe that a reasonable expectation for weight loss is a few pounds a week on a consistent basis.

The clinician who works with habit disorder patients would do well to examine his own beliefs about the problem he is treating, specifically the notions of addiction and dependency. It is certainly helpful to review the current literature in this field, especially in relationship to alcohol and nicotine problems. However, the principles of Ericksonian hypnotherapy provide strong guidance in leading the therapist to deal with the patient's own beliefs, which must be understood and paced in order to effect change.

CHAPTER 8

VARIABLES FOR SUCCESS

SO FAR, WE HAVE surveyed the important concepts and techniques of modern hypnosis as applied to habit disorders. Now, let's put it all together. Positive results depend on much more than a thorough knowledge and skill in using all of the individual concepts and techniques. In this chapter, we will discuss how we typically structure and organize our treatment of habit disorders. Case studies in the next chapter further clarify our organization of treatment. This chapter will also present some important variables that need to be taken into consideration in order to achieve treatment success.

THE STRUCTURE OF TREATMENT

The treatment of patients with habit disorders is always unique, depending on the characteristics of the individual. Group treatment cannot pace or utilize the uniqueness of each person, so the success of group treatment will always be lower. However, after individualized intervention has helped patients to find healthier patterns of behavior, group treatment may be in order primarily as a cost-effective supportive measure.

Even though our treatment is individualized, it usually is structured as follows:

A. The Initial Communication
   1. Fees and screening
   2. Generating treatment potentials

B. Formal Treatment
  1. Gather relevant data and pace
  2. Formal hypnotic communication (reframing, anchoring, imagery, direct and indirect suggestions)
  3. Self-hypnosis and other directives
C. Post-treatment Strategies
  1. Self-hypnosis
  2. Utilizing other resources

THE INITIAL COMMUNICATION

The initial communication with a patient will usually be over the telephone. Because these calls are so important, we recommend that, whenever possible, *the clinician speak personally to the patient*. If not, the interviewer should be an assistant well trained in how to handle such situations.

Telephone communication is an opportunity to generate an initial pace with prospective patients and to set up positive treatment potentials. For example, at times we have described our reframing orientation to a prospective patient. Here's an example:

> I'll rarely use aversive communication or suggestions like telling you sweets will taste like something you hate. Instead, I'm very respectful of whatever benefits or payoffs you've gotten from overeating. My approach is to help you find alternatives that are healthier and perhaps even more satisfying for you.

In every case where we have communicated this over the telephone, it has been well received.

Often prospective patients are "shopping around" or desire information only. Such patients greatly appreciate talking personally to the clinician; this also significantly increases the probability of their making an appointment, assuming that they are not screened out by the clinician as inappropriate candidates for treatment. Patients desiring information frequently ask specific questions requiring the clinician's knowledge and skill.

An issue that frequently arises over the telephone during the initial contact is the patient's misconceptions and consequent anxiety regarding hypnosis and trance. We will frequently clarify and demystify what hypnosis is over the phone and assure the prospective patient that time will be taken during the initial treatment session to fully orient him or her to hypnosis and trance.

To many prospective patients we indicate that, although hypnosis is one of our primary treatment modalities and has been very effective in dealing with their particular disorder, we will only be able to judge how appropriate its use would be after the first session. This allows the therapist the necessary flexibility to use other forms of strategic intervention.

General information regarding fees or treatment can be given to others, but *the prospective patient must request the appointment.* Sometimes we will make a tentative appointment with a family member or friend, but the patient must call and confirm. Only in this way can we gather the necessary screening data. Someone else's calling for an appointment is a strong indicator of patient resistance and greatly increases the probability of treatment failure. Exceptions to this policy are made only for children under 12 or persons who are mute.

FEES

Charging fees can serve two important purposes as far as treatment is concerned: 1) It screens out persons who are not sufficiently motivated for treatment, and 2) it can enhance the patient's motivation once money is paid. For these reasons (and because we like to make a nice living), our fees are relatively high. This is particularly true for smokers, who are charged up to $300.00 for our "one-shot" two-hour session. This fee for smokers includes a one-hour booster follow-up, if needed, at no additional cost; however, we do not tell this to patients because it will "suggest" to them the need for follow-up work which is not usually required. Since it would be counter-therapeutic to share this with the patient, the fees may seem artificially high, but for those who need the extra hour the fees are only slightly higher than our hourly rate. Another reason not to tell patients about this extra session is that, for those who need it because they have not totally stopped smoking, the fact that this session is free dissipates some of their anger and increases their cooperation during this extra session. When the costs of an unhealthy habit – physical, psychological, and social – are considered, our fees are not that high. An average smoker will spend our fee on cigarettes in four or five months.

Cigarette smokers must send a deposit of $150.00 before an appointment is scheduled. The balance is due on the date of treatment. One author requires the entire fee in advance. Before we instituted this policy many patients did not show up for scheduled appointments, often without cancelling. The deposit serves as a commitment on the patient's part to make the appointment. Occasionally, we have requested initial deposits from patients other than smokers. We tell patients who are accepted for treatment to think about it and, when they're ready to make a commitment, to put a check in the mail.

For less financially able patients, we have a schedule of sliding fees. However, part of the socialization process in our capitalistic society is the message that "you get nothing for free." Consequently, patients offered free treatment have very low expectations. For that reason, as well as to increase motivation, we believe that it is important that all patients pay at least *something* out of their own pockets.

SCREENING PROSPECTIVE PATIENTS

Because our intervention is generally short-term (a "one-shot" two- to three-hour treatment for most smokers, an average of five to seven hourly sessions for most overweight patients, and about seven to ten hourly sessions for alcoholics), we carefully screen over the phone for patients who are not appropriate for treatment. Even though they occur, we don't like treatment failures; screening is an important way to increase the probability of success. We turn down about 20% of the people who call us for treatment, but in many cases suggest that those persons inquire again at a later date. Our experience is that in almost all situations the caller appreciates our honesty and professional integrity; also, many of these persons call back when conditions are more appropriate for treatment.

Keep in mind that the better you screen, the more successful you'll be. And there is no better testimonial to your professionalism than an ex-smoker, a slender person who previously was heavy or obese, or a recovering and sober alcoholic. More importantly, we want to do whatever we can to prevent a patient from feeling like a failure.

Those variables that we have found important to consider for screening purposes are discussed below. Since the screening process involves collecting personal information over the phone, we always tell the caller to let us know if he or she wishes to keep any of the requested data private. The data collected are used not only to select appropriate treatment candidates but also to plan the initial treatment strategies for those patients we do accept.

1) Current Life Stress

Cigarettes, food and alcohol are commonly used to deal with stress. Therefore, if the caller has recently or is currently experiencing extraordinary stress (e.g., death of a loved one, separation or divorce, a job change, college exams), it is often wise to request that the person wait until the stress has diminished. The exception to this might be in the case of problem drinkers or other patients with significant medical needs. Very often, drinking causes more problems, exacerbating stress, and the drinker is stuck in a vicious circle until drinking ceases.

2) Reasons Why the Caller Is Seeking Treatment Now

We always ask the caller, "Why now? Why not six months ago? Why not next year?" The responses to this inquiry often provide valuable clues as to the motivation of the caller. We also ask, "Is anyone bugging or pushing you to seek treatment?" Beware of the caller seeking treatment *primarily* to make someone else happy! Because of the resistance that will be involved (remember, passive stubbornness or a need to assert one's independence is a common payoff for unhealthy habits), such situations are almost sure to lead to treatment failure. Very often, callers will say that loved ones or friends have expressed concern, and this is acceptable as long as the caller is also very motivated. By the way, we do not expect prospective patients to be 100% motivated to give up an unhealthy habit. If that were the case, then by definition the person would stop. Many callers will admit to not being totally motivated or will be aware of a "part" that loves a cigarette, sweets, or a drink. Of course, that is the "part" of the person that we most especially communicate with during hypnotic treatment.

Quite often, a crisis associated with an unhealthy habit is the factor that has motivated a caller to seek treatment. Such crises might be recently diagnosed health problems (e.g., emphysema, hypertension, liver disorders) or psychosocial crises (e.g., assaultive behavior or auto accidents associated with alcoholism). These are frequently positive factors in terms of motivating patients to seek treatment. In fact, our clinical strategy has at times included "precipitating a crisis" (e.g., telling a wife to leave an alcoholic husband) in order to generate motivation for changes in behavior or for treatment. Beware of the prospective patient who seeks treatment only so you will write a letter to a judge or employer and who intends to leave treatment and engage in the unhealthy habit again as soon as the "heat is off"! Always remember—you can't save everyone. Put your energy where you can make a difference.

3) Past or Current Emotional Difficulties

During screening, we will assess any past or current emotional difficulties. This information can usually be elicited by asking the prospective patient if he or she in the past received or is currently undergoing treatment for any major emotional disorders. Our concern here is primarily to screen out patients currently suffering from significant emotional illness (e.g., schizophrenia and manic depression) because of the strong possibility that they are relying on an unhealthy habit to deal with significant emotional distress (i.e., self-tranquilization).

At times, we will see patients currently undergoing counseling or psychotherapy with someone else and consider our treatment as an adjunctive intervention. It is not uncommon to find that, when such patients utilize their inner power and resources to stop smoking, overeating, or drinking, other problems disappear or are significantly alleviated. When we accept for treatment a patient currently in counseling, we request that the patient inform the counselor or therapist and sometimes we will talk to the other therapist first to obtain helpful data.

4) Past Treatment History

Mark Twain once said, "I'm an expert at not smoking. I've stopped a thousand times." Twain would have been a very poor candidate for the treatment of his cigarette habit. Be wary of the motivation of the prospective patient who has stopped smoking, dieted, or been "on the wagon" many times, especially if such attempts were in the recent past and if the abstinence was short-lived. Some patients will be out to put you and hypnotic treatment on their "hit list" of clinicians and therapeutic modalities they've tried. Then such patients can say to themselves or others, "I even tried hypnosis and that didn't work."

On the other hand, a positive sign is a recent attempt at cessation or modification of an unhealthy habit that was sustained for any reasonable length of time, especially if the patient acted without therapeutic intervention or support.

One thing we make clear to patients during our initial communication is that hypnosis is not magic, but rather an effective clinical procedure. It works best for people who have been able to do some work by themselves but for some reason just can't seem to get "over the hump." We tell patients that our greatest successes in the past have been with those people who tell us that they can do 80% by themselves — for example, dieters who eat properly all day but have problems controlling themselves at night watching television, or smokers who have quit a few times for a couple of weeks but then given in again to that craving. These patients are highly likely to be successful. If a prospective patient has not even tried to change the behavior by himself, the prognosis is poor.

If the prospective patient has failed at past hypnotic intervention, we obtain data on the exact nature of the hypnotic treatment so that we can avoid doing the same thing. We are more likely to accept such patients if they have experienced group hypnosis or hypnotic intervention which relied primarily on aversive suggestions, since our treatment is in such contrast to these styles.

5) For Cigarette Smokers, the Extent of Alcohol Use

For many cigarette users, alcohol is a powerful anchor that elicits cigarette smoking. Furthermore, alcohol use lowers inhibitions of persons attempting not to smoke. Therefore, we carefully gather data on alcohol use from persons inquiring about treatment for smoking. Simply asking such persons how much they drink tends to elicit vague responses (e.g., "socially," "just now and then"). We ask callers when they last had any kind of alcohol and how much, and the last time before that, and the last time prior to that. We will usually refuse treatment to smokers who are heavy drinkers until they have first cut down their ingestion of alcohol. Further, we will insist that problem drinkers maintain sobriety for at least one year before treating them for other habit disorders.

6) The Current Extent of the Habit

Questions about the current extent of the problem are asked primarily of callers who want to lose weight. We refuse such treatment to anyone less than 10 pounds overweight for several reasons. First, we do not want to reinforce an unwarranted or obsessive preoccupation with being overweight. Secondly, the probability of treatment success with such persons is significantly lower than with more overweight patients. However, at times we will suggest that callers who sound preoccupied with their weight obtain treatment for that obsession. This latter group includes persons who alternate between binging and restrictive diets, and those who binge and then purge (bulimics).

Alcoholism is a complex phenomenon that is difficult to define precisely. Jellinek's typology of five types (1960) is still mentioned at times;* however, most people familiar with the field agree that there is great variability in alcoholic behavior. We believe that it is best to define alcoholism as *drinking that the patient cannot control*, even if it is periodic drinking, especially if it is causing or associated with ongoing dysfunction. The dysfunction could be physical (e.g., chronic gastritis or liver disorders), psychosocial (e.g., poor interpersonal relationship or job performance problems), or legal (e.g., DWI arrests, auto accidents).

We have rarely received treatment inquiries from smokers using less than about 15 cigarettes daily. In cases where the caller smokes fewer than 15 cigarettes a day, we suggest that the caller attempt to quit on his or her own first. With extremely heavy smokers (i.e., four or more packs daily), we will often request the caller to reduce intake to two packs or less and to call us back at that time. We believe that if heavy smokers are highly motivated, they can accomplish this much on their own.

7) The Longevity of the Habit

Since the vast majority of smokers begin to smoke in their teen years or early twenties, for smokers this variable usually correlates with their age. And, as is the case with most habits, the longer a person has relied on cigarettes, or the older the person is, the more challenging it will be to stop. Counterbalancing the longevity factor in elderly smokers, however, is the frequent occurrence of imminent or ongoing health problems (e.g., emphysema or cardiovascular symptoms), which can greatly moti-

---

*Jellinek's five types of alcoholism are Alpha, Beta, Gamma, Delta and Epsilon. Alpha alcoholics are psychologically but not physically dependent on alcohol. Jellinek characterized Beta alcoholics as suffering from nutritional deficiency disease associated with drinking. Gamma alcoholism (thought by Jellinek to be the most prevalent type in American society) is defined by the *loss of control* phenomenon — an ability to abstain from drinking on occasions but a lack of control over intake once drinking has begun. The Delta alcoholic is a so-called steady-state drinker who maintains a relatively even blood alcohol concentration through the day. Finally, the Epsilon alcoholic is the periodic drinker who is subject to unpredictable binges after days, weeks or months.

vate these patients. Even so, we usually plan more sessions than our typical "one-shot" treatment for elderly smokers.

Persons who have had poor eating habits and have been overweight consistently since childhood are extremely challenging patients. It usually will require a great deal of therapeutic skill and support to help these patients deal with themselves and the world as people of normal weight. These patients, as well as those who were overweight before or during their teen years, tend to hold on to a body image of themselves as heavy even as they lose weight and appear smaller or more slender to others. Their poor body image diminishes the reinforcement of losing the weight that is so helpful for others and can sabotage progress.

The longevity of alcoholism is generally correlated with more challenging treatment. However, it is often impossible to compute longevity due to the difficulty in determining precisely where social or controlled drinking ended and problem drinking or alcoholism began. Treatment of patients with histories of consistent heavy drinking for many years and with no periods of sobriety or controlled drinking can be extremely difficult, and relapse is probable. However, keep in mind that for most alcoholics the normal course of recovery, defined in terms of long-term sobriety, includes a number of relapses. The therapist should also be aware of a "telescoping" tendency for the development of alcoholism in women; that is, many women display alcoholic behavior within a much shorter time span than most men, sometimes in a few years instead of many.

8) Other Data

Included here is age, employment, marital status and children, and data on other persons living in the same household (including whether they suffer from any habit disorders). Such data will usually not be as useful for screening as some variables discussed earlier. However, data in this category have at times tipped the scale in one direction or the other in terms of our deciding to treat someone. For example, these data give us an indication of the supportive resources of the prospective patient;

generally speaking, the more resources that are available, the higher the probability of treatment success. An alcoholic with a family and job is a better treatment candidate than an unemployed single alcoholic. An executive with a "pressure cooker" job will not be as good a candidate for treatment to stop smoking as a part-time nurse who is a "happy-go-lucky" type person and reports feeling quite satisfied with her life.

UTILIZING ALL OPPORTUNITIES TO POTENTIATE TREATMENT

In earlier chapters we have presented many different ways to communicate effectively with patients and, thus, to increase the probability of treatment success. We do our best to make *all* of our communications to patients purposeful, from the initial call to the termination of treatment. As was pointed out in Chapter 4, even while our patients sit in a waiting room, we look for ways to potentiate their treatment—for example, by talking to someone else or by talking into the phone while they are listening. After our initial treatment for weight loss, as we are walking someone out the door, our last communication will often be this humorous but purposeful comment: "I'll expect to see a little less of you when I see you next time." We have even utilized answering machines to generate positive treatment potentials, as illustrated by this message one of us recently used, "I've just returned from vacation so I'm ready to do good work for you."

A powerful form of communication and an important learning strategy is *modeling*. We believe that it is incongruent communication and poor modeling for any health professional to have ashtrays in the work setting. Of course, this is even more ridiculous if you are treating smokers. The same applies if you are very overweight and helping others to lose weight. A favorite saying of ours is, "You shouldn't be a plumber in someone else's house until you get your own sink unclogged." We realize that this statement is controversial; however, most of the protests will come from unhealthy health professionals.

SPECIFIC TREATMENT ASPECTS

Cigarette Smokers

Treatment for most cigarette smokers consists of a one-shot two-hour long session. Unlike eating, which is a necessity for survival, smoking is never necessary. When we indicate that one hypnotic session can completely eliminate the habit, the power of the treatment is intensified because of the increased expectations of the patient. Therefore, we set up as many positive treatment potentials as possible before this session (over the phone and through correspondence) by framing this one session as a very important event for the patient. We do whatever we can to help the person to *never* smoke again after treatment. Even though we are presenting a one-shot treatment model, we maintain a flexible approach. Occasionally, when clinical judgment indicates, we will contract for multi-session treatment.

The first thing we do after the patient comes into the office is usually some form of ritual during which the patient says goodbye to any cigarettes he has. One of the authors actually requests his patients to bring in "the last cigarette" and the patient is given the choice of smoking it (the only time anyone is allowed to smoke in the office) or throwing it away. The other authors simply ask the patient if she has any cigarettes, and if so, the patient is invited to toss them in the trash can.

The next 30 to 60 minutes are spent obtaining a history and other relevant data. Many of the questions we ask are similar to or the same as those asked during screening (previously described in this chapter) but in more depth. We always inquire as to the onset of cigarette smoking and the contexts during which smoking behavior is elicited. We ask about family members who smoked or currently smoke, even grandparents, and the quality of the relationship with those persons. We ask questions about what's stressful and what's fun and generally do our best to get to know the patient. Throughout this data collection process, we do whatever we can to pace the patient and to utilize opportunities to communicate effectively. For example, we may spontaneously tell some stories (therapeutic metaphors) in reaction to things the patient says, and we always refer to the patient's cigarette habit in the past tense (e.g., "Please tell me about the situations which, in the past, prompted you to smoke.").

After gathering data and getting into pace with the patient, we educate our patient about hypnosis and trance (see Chapter 1) and answer any questions about these subjects. Keep in mind that patients often go into trance when you're talking about it, and it can be helpful to point that out to them at the time.

After clarifying hypnosis and trance, the formal work begins. Often we ask the patient to sit in the "trance chair"; then we start with a structured induction (e.g., counting numbers on an imaginary chalkboard or staring at something and closing the eyelids slowly or imagining oneself descending in an elevator floor by floor) which in our clinical judgment is suitable for the patient. For example, a kinesthetic induction such as imagining oneself descending in an elevator may be a more suitable induction for a poor visualizer than imagining a chalkboard and numbers. The structured induction gives the patient an induction to use for self-hypnosis later. Next, we use an Ericksonian conversational induction (see Erickson, Rossi, and Rossi, 1976) to deepen trance and set up potentials for new learning. Treatment then usually consists of reframing, anchoring, imagery, and indirect and direct suggestions. Finally, the formal hypnotic session will usually end with instructions and suggestions to use self-hypnosis and, in "one-shot" sessions, the directive to call in one week "to say how *well* you're doing."

Overweight Patients

Our treatment of these patients has averaged about five to seven hourly sessions. The first session, however, is sometimes scheduled for one and a half hours. As mentioned earlier, cigarette users can stop smoking altogether and, of course, be healthier. But since everyone must eat, overweight patients usually need ongoing support while healthier patterns are established. The second session for these patients will almost always be about a week after the first. After that, the sessions can be weekly or every two to three weeks, depending on the patient's need for structure and support.

Sometimes potent emotional conflicts associated with losing weight arise, and clinical hypnotists should be prepared to deal with such matters. For example, many overweight patients are frightened about dealing with some intimate interpersonal issues they perceive as more threatening if they lose weight and are more physically attractive. For some overweight patients the reframing process can take months as they experiment with alternatives to overeating or to being overweight. Often this process requires therapeutic input and support.

Overweight patients are told ahead of time to come in for their first treatment session with a healthy diet "that will work for you" and a plan of healthy exercise to use for 30 or more minutes a day, three to five days a week. Our experience is that most patients know more about dieting than we do. They have already "tried" many different ones and know what they can stick to best. Each of us has a nutritionist to whom we can refer patients for consultation, but such consultations are rarely needed. Health professionals in agency and institutional settings may find it necessary to familiarize themselves with some dietary plans to suggest to their patients.

Most of the first treatment session is spent obtaining a history and other relevant data and getting into pace with the patient. Next, we inquire as to the diet and exercise plan chosen by the patient and we will make any modifications we feel are helpful. We will suggest 30 to 60 minutes of exercise three to five days a week (occasionally six days a week). The number of days of exercise a week is usually based on such variables as the current health and age of the patient and our clinical intuition as to just how much discipline will be most therapeutic for a particular person. Usually we also discuss the rationale for exercising (i.e., to help burn off calories and to counteract a bodily homeostatic tendency to slow down metabolism as caloric intake decreases).

Overweight patients are instructed to weigh themselves on the same scale *only once a week* (in some cases twice a week), on the same day each week. Of course, this is to prevent obsessively stepping on the scale and consequent disappointment when there is no reduction or when there are slight increases due to metabolic changes.

If time permits during the first session, hypnosis and trance are clarified, and the patient is helped to experience trance by using a structured induction followed by some conversational patter and suggestions for self-hypnosis. The session ends with a contract for dieting, exercise, daily self-hypnosis, and a specified weight loss by the next session. Even when there is no time for hypnotic work, a contract for dieting, exercise and weight loss by the second session is agreed upon. We tell patients that they can take off a few pounds by themselves to "get started" before we begin our hypnotic work. Patients rarely disagree with this. It is our experience that it generally paces these patients to initially provide a good bit of structure and to be relatively firm but reasonable in our expectations.

The second session is seven to ten days later. At that time, we monitor the patient's progress and suggest any necessary modifications to diet, exercise or the use of self-hypnosis. Treatment proceeds with reframing, anchoring, and other hypnotic work.

Later treatment sessions with overweight patients are sometimes spent primarily in monitoring progress, directly discussing changes taking place in the patient's life, and providing supportive hypnotic communication. Especially in the beginning of therapy, many overweight patients find it very helpful to receive ongoing support and to know that they must "check in" with the therapist. Toward the end of therapy, we "wean" patients by increasing the time between treatment sessions.

Alcoholics

When there is evidence of physical dependence on alcohol, patients are told that they must undergo detoxification before we will proceed with hypnosis. This usually takes place in an inpatient setting. The first hypnosis session is scheduled as soon as possible after completion of the detoxification treatment, and patients are told ahead of time that the objective of treatment will be to maintain sobriety.

The first appointment is often one and a half hours. Along with the patient, close family members and other persons living in the household are requested to come to the first session. This includes any preadolescent or adolescent children. To begin this session everyone shares perceptions about the problem. Typically, we then enlist everyone's support and cooperation with treatment. Sometimes a discussion will take place about any possible roles those present may have played (usually unconsciously) in promoting alcoholic behavior. For example, we may point out any evidence of consistent "rescuing" of the alcoholic and how such patterns may actually be reinforcing alcoholic behavior. Very often, other persons close to the patient are told that a firm approach is likely to help the patient the most. Finally, a recommendation is frequently made that family members attend support and educational programs such as Alanon and Alateen. The first session continues with our providing some educational data about alcoholism, usually focusing on why sobriety has been found to be the best objective (as opposed to social or controlled drinking, which the majority of alcoholics cannot accomplish for any extended period of time). With everyone present, the patient is requested to make a commitment to be sober for some particular length of time suggested by the therapist, usually from three months to a year. It is strongly hinted that at the end of that period the patient can make another commitment. Such commitments, of course, are very similar to the Alcoholics Anonymous objective of "one day at a time." The suggested time commitment we choose is based on a variety of factors, including the type of alcoholic behavior that the patient has displayed (e.g., we would suggest a longer time commitment for the episodic drinker who has a history of binges only once every few months). Sometimes the sobriety time commitment might have some metaphoric meaning. For example, one author recently suggested a nine-month sobriety commitment when he perceived that a subtle but powerful issue for the alcoholic patient and his wife was whether or not to have a child.

As treatment proceeds with the patient only, hypnosis and trance are clarified. After a structured induction and then a conversational induction, we proceed with reframing, anchoring, a variety of hypnotic suggestions and instructions for self-hypnosis. Often we must wait until later sessions to complete reframing and anchoring. In most cases, we strongly recommend that alcoholic patients attend AA. Sometimes patients need coaxing or some firm direction because of hesitancy about AA; at times we direct hesitant patients to attend at least three or four meetings to find out firsthand how AA can be of value to them. Especially in major metropolitan areas, there are many AA meetings at different times of the day and in different locations. Sometimes patients will feel more comfortable with some AA groups than with others. Attending various meetings at the outset in order to find a group that feels comfortable can often be beneficial for a patient. Frequently, AA serves as a healthy alternative to drinking or to the bar scene in terms of the support and companionship AA offers and also as a way to pass time. It is interesting that the Eleventh Step* of the "Twelve Steps" of AA mentions "meditation." This orientation can help AA members to accept hypnosis and self-hypnosis as treatment strategies.

SELF-HYPNOSIS

Virtually all of the patients we see are instructed in the use of self-hypnosis and we will usually direct the patient to begin using this tool from the beginning of treatment. Much of our rationale for this has already been explained in Chapter 5. The use of self-hypnosis gives our patients the opportunity to have an active role in their own treatment and in keeping themselves healthy.

---

*The Eleventh Step of Alcoholics Anonymous: "Sought through prayer and meditation to improve our conscious contact with God as we understood Him, praying only for knowledge of His will for us and the power to carry that out."

RELAPSE OF SYMPTOMS

Relapses to the old unhealthy habit or patterns of behavior need to be handled on an individual basis. Sometimes a supportive approach is best and in those cases we do what's necessary to boost the patient's confidence and motivation again. An explanation that a relapse or "regression" is common during growth can often take away the stigma of failure, as well as helping the patient to learn from the relapse in order to do better in the future.

Of course, some patients may require more firmness if that paces their personality and if there are indications that they did not follow through on responsibilities (e.g., by ignoring important directives). In some cases we have had to terminate treatment when there was sufficient evidence that the patient was continuing to not carry out certain responsibilities.

Quite often, of course, relapses are signals to the therapist that something important was not addressed in treatment. In such cases, the therapist should explore (through reframing) any payoffs or benefits that are not being taken care of by alternatives to the unhealthy habit. Many of the techniques already discussed in this book are useful strategies in preventing symptom relapses. These include regular use of self-hypnosis, posthypnotic suggestions for the unconscious to reframe when necessary in the future, and prescribing symptom relapses during treatment and follow-up.

UTILIZING OTHER RESOURCES

We very much believe in utilizing all resources that might further treatment. People close to the patient are sometimes invited to sessions so that we can hear their perceptions of the situation and enlist their support. As already mentioned, we direct most alcoholic patients to look into Alcoholic Anonymous and we suggest groups like Alanon to family members. We also support groups like Overeaters Anonymous and groups for ex-smokers that are often sponsored by local chapters of the American Cancer Society or the American Lung Association. All of these groups can be utilized as adjuncts to individual treatment and as post-treatment support.

This chapter has presented the structure and organization of techniques we typically use in the hypnotherapeutic treatment of habit disorders. We have also presented some other important variables for treatment success. To be successful a good workman must not only have the right tools but must also know how, when, and where to use them.

CHAPTER 9

CASE STUDIES

THE FOLLOWING CASE studies illustrate many of the hypnotic techniques discussed in this book. These case studies are compiled from our own clinical notes and point out some of the common dynamics and issues that arise in the treatment of habit disorders. In order to maintain a clinical flavor, the first person singular is used in presenting these cases.

CAROL – SMOKING

Carol was a 54-year-old married woman with three grown children and two grandchildren. She described her marriage as good but with its "ups and downs." Carol's husband was a busy and successful executive. She stated that in prior years it had been a challenge to adapt to the fact that he spent so much time working and that his "workaholism" had been an issue that caused tension in their marriage. However, she said that she had learned to live with his busy schedule and felt good about the "nice things in our marriage." Carol's main activities consisted of maintaining the home, in which she was assisted by a maid, and being a socialite of sorts. In that regard, she entertained mutual friends and her husband's business associates.

Carol said that her husband had never smoked and that at times "he bugs me about my cigarettes, but I want to stop myself." Carol's mother died at the age of 66 from advanced emphysema and her father died at the age of 70 from a heart attack. She stated that a sister, 61 years old, had recently died from emphysema and that this condition runs in her family. She stated that she was recently diagnosed as having the beginning signs of emphysema, and that the doctors told her that she must stop smoking or it "would kill me." She stated that this was why she had come for treatment.

She stated candidly, "There is a part of me that loves cigarettes, but in other ways I hate them." When I asked her what that part of her loved about cigarettes, she stated, "They have been my friend and my companion; they give me warmth and comfort." She said she hated cigarettes because, "They're dirty and unhealthy and smell foul." She stated, "I *must* stop smoking cigarettes."

Carol began smoking cigarettes when she was 16 years old. She was graduated from high school and went two years to a "finishing school" before meeting and marrying her husband. She stopped smoking totally during the pregnancies of her last two children and said that she smoked only now and then when she was pregnant with her first child. She had stopped smoking for a few weeks on two other occasions when she had been sick and had attempted to quit.

Carol came in for a one-shot two-hour treatment session. During the data collection phase of the session, Carol was very poised and articulate, and seemed to have a great deal of energy. She was enthusiastic as she talked and gestured with her hands and arms quite a bit. Other than the early symptoms of emphysema, Carol was in good health. She was taking no other medication, and the only alcohol she consumed was one or two drinks every few weeks at a cocktail party and one or two glasses of wine with dinner once or twice a week. Carol stated that she had read many things about hypnosis, had taken a course in self-hypnosis, and that she believed in it very much. She stated that she had never been formally hypnotized.

While I was clarifying trance and hypnosis to Carol, she interrupted with the statement, "I do that all the time." When I asked her what she meant, she stated that she had just become aware that she had spontaneously gone into trance for years whenever she was bored with a conversation or other kinds of events that were going on around her and wanted to "tune something out." When I asked her if she would be willing to demonstrate, she agreed, shifted her body, and stared straight off into space with her eyes open. It was quite apparent that she was in trance. I remarked that she certainly did know how to experience trance and that this ability would help our work.

By the time Carol moved to the "trance chair," I felt that we had established a strong pace with each other. Before formal hypnotic induction, I told Carol that I wanted to teach her a relaxation strategy that was going to be helpful. This consisted of her pushing her thumb to her middle or index finger (she chose the index finger) as she slowly took a deep breath of air, and when she exhaled her breath, to quickly let go of the tension in her fingers and arms which was produced by pushing her fingers together. I asked Carol if she could think of a word or phrase that she could say to herself as she exhaled and let go that would symbolize comfort and letting go to her. After a few moments, she said "fog" and explained that several times in her life she had been out in the fog and that it was a very comfortable, warm experience for her, something that at times she daydreamed about in a comfortable way. I suggested to Carol that the thumb and breathing exercise would serve as a strategic technique to feel relaxed or posed. (This technique utilizes the principles of anchoring described in Chapter 3). After Carol did the finger and breathing exercise a few times, I asked her to let herself go into trance as she had done many times before by just staring off into space. I said that her eyes could stay open or closed; after a few moments she closed her eyes. I continued to communicate to her hypnotically to deepen trance and to set up therapeutic potentials. During the induction I made reference to the beach and reminded Carol of all the times she had sunned herself on the beach and "felt that natural warmth and comfort." I also suggested that she might "wonder about other wonderful healthy ways to get warmth and comfort." The objective here was to pace Carol using her own words describing what she loved about cigarettes, and then to remind her of her own history in finding warmth and comfort in natural healthy ways and to suggest to her still other ways to get what she needs.

During the initial steps of reframing, I told Carol the metaphorical story about my resistance in completing my doctoral dissertation because my father "bugged me" about it. This was intended to pace and depotentiate any resistance that may have

p. 130.

been generated by her husband's "bugging" her about cigarettes. (This story is told in Chapter 6. In the story told to Carol, "father" was used instead of "mother" to more closely parallel Carol's situation.) When I asked Carol to consciously experience that part of her that was responsible for her smoking cigarettes, she reported seeing an image in her mind of herself as a little girl. She said the little girl was crying and angry because she couldn't get her way. When we were discussing payoffs during reframing, I mentioned that it was likely that two important and related payoffs she got from smoking cigarettes were that a cigarette was a "friend and companion to her" and that a cigarette gave her "warmth and comfort" whenever she needed that. Again, in order to pace her, I used the same words that Carol had communicated previously, and Carol's nonverbal minimal cues (nodding her head) affirmed that these were important payoffs for her from cigarettes. At my request, she identified these other payoffs that she had gotten from cigarettes: 1) "something to do with my hands," 2) "to help me feel poised and in control when I'm with other people," and 3) "after dinner it's the time to shift from eating any more" (so she wouldn't get overweight) "and to take a break."

Carol began to cry as I mentioned that healthier alternatives to cigarettes were available to her. She volunteered that she began to feel very sad that she had continued to blame her husband for depriving her of attention because of time he devoted to his work. She explained that in recent years he had spent increasingly more time with her and that he "really was a good husband. . . . I've always been spoiled." Carol then began to feel better and reported a new perspective and feeling of appreciation for her husband. She also decided to rely more on other people, like her children, grandchildren, and close friends, if she felt a need for "companionship, warmth or comfort."

At my suggestion, Carol decided to use the thumb-to-finger relaxation technique as an alternative to cigarette smoking for something to do with her hands and to feel poised in social situations. She also decided to knit, which she had done years earlier, to give her something to do with her hands. Carol became aware that the thumb-to-finger technique and/or knitting would also be nice alternatives to cigarettes to help her shift from eating to relaxing or some other activity.

After her alternatives were checked out and found to be acceptable, I asked Carol to remember an experience that she had any time at all in her life when she felt very strong, poised, powerful and in control. When she accessed that memory, I set up an anchor for those inner kinesthetic experiences by firmly grasping her left hand. To future pace Carol, this anchor was fired (see Chapter 3) as she was asked to imagine the following future experiences: walking into her house later that afternoon, the end of dinner that evening, the next morning as she drank her coffee, an evening when she was home alone and her husband was working late, and herself walking into a cocktail party.

After the reframing, Carol and "all parts of her" were thanked for the good work she had done and I continued to communicate hypnotically. I told Carol how I had recently run into my friend Karen (this name was purposely chosen because of its similarity to the patient's name) who told me about a problem that she had been having. I then told her the story of my friend who had difficulty when men wanted to have sex with her. (This metaphoric story is described in Chapter 4.) I continued with the following metaphorical communication:

> You know, Carol, I often look out of this window and observe what's going on out there. This morning I noticed a woman walking down the street with three little children who were quite young. (*This was a pace for the patient and her three children.*) I noticed that the lady stepped off the sidewalk to say hello to someone and when she did the three kids stepped off the sidewalk into the gutter in the street and started playing with some mud and trash that was lying there. I heard the mother yell, "*Don't do that (an embedded suggestion)*; that's dirty and smells foul, and it's unhealthy to play with that and you shouldn't be in the street anyway." (*These words describe how some part of the patient has felt about cigarettes and therefore paced her.*) I saw that mother round up the

three kids and bring them over to the safety of the sidewalk, even though they screamed and protested and obviously felt deprived (*the word the patient used to describe how some part of her felt at times*). You know, I'll bet in some kind of way those little kids really appreciated that mother looking after them.

Next, I talked to Carol about the common experience of having a longtime friend and companion who often provides warmth and comfort (words that Carol used to describe cigarettes), but finding out some things about that friend that aren't healthy or positive for us. (See the "friendly enemy" story in Chapter 4.) I continued by talking about how sad it can be to "*say goodbye to that enemy in disguise*, Carol" (an embedded suggestion), and I stated my guess that Carol had probably had that experience in her life. (Carol nodded affirmatively.)

Next, I suggested to the patient that she do self-hypnosis daily for 10 minutes or more for 30 days and then at least three or four times a week thereafter. I also suggested that she practice the finger and breathing exercise 10 times or more daily and to use it whenever needed. Here is a transcript of my communication to her:

> Carol, for the next 30 days I want to suggest to you that every day for a minimum of 10 minutes you sit down in a comfortable chair and use that thumb-to-finger and breathing technique a few times, and then let yourself go into trance. Just experience trance for 10 minutes or longer. Your trance will be a signal to your unconscious to continue to help you out with all its power and all its resources. I also want to suggest that at least 10 times daily for the next month, and whenever you need it, that you use that finger and breathing technique. Carol, your unconscious has all the tools you'll need. It has all the dials *to tune in, Carol, whatever is nice for you* (an embedded suggestion using the language that paced Carol) and *to tune out what you don't need to hear or listen to* (an em-

bedded suggestion). Your unconscious mind has so much data, everything you've seen and heard and felt in your life. It's all there just as data to put together for whatever new ways of perceiving and experiencing, that will help you out (*this essentially describes the reframing process*).

After some messages for hypnotic amnesia (so that Carol would not remember and therefore analyze and possibly generate resistance to the work we had done), Carol alerted and reoriented at my suggestion.

At my request, Carol called me a week later and said that things were going well for her. At my request also, she called me one month after that and stated that she was still not smoking, that she and her husband were getting along better than they had in years, and that she was using self-hypnosis and the finger and breathing technique regularly.

MOLLY—OVERWEIGHT

Molly was a 34-year-old divorced woman who came into therapy to work on a weight problem. Molly saw herself as 20 to 25 pounds overweight. Most of this weight gain had occurred in the prior three years. Besides the obvious health issues involved with carrying too much weight around, Molly had a problem peculiar to her profession. Molly was a local TV personality, doing feature stories on the news and on a local talk show. She saw, probably accurately, a very nice physical appearance as being essential to maintaining her job.

In taking her family history, we learned that her mother had gained a significant amount of weight in her mid-thirties and kept it on for the rest of her life. She had a serious stroke at age 58 and died at age 61, just two years before Molly entered therapy. Except for emphysema from smoking, her father was in good health. Her only sibling, a younger sister, had no significant medical problems that Molly knew about and was not overweight.

The first session was used to gather data and discuss hypnosis and trance with Molly. Molly was in good health, with a history of minor surgery five years previously. Until age 30, Molly had been able to keep her weight in the slender-to-moderate range with little effort. However, during the past three to four years (and especially during the past year) she had experienced significant weight gain.

Molly had married a childhood sweetheart at age 27 and they divorced three years later. Molly reported that the divorce was "not her idea," that it was very "traumatic for me," and that she had no plans to ever get married again.

Molly had moved to her present city upon securing a job approximately three years earlier. She liked the city and had a number of good friends, both male and female, but had not dated anyone seriously since her divorce.

Molly claimed that she could do a good job on her own, watching her weight all day long, but experienced significant difficulty in the evening while reading or watching TV. The weekends were also very problematic for her. She claimed that exercise was "a four-letter word," her biggest objection being that "it bores me."

After collecting the intake data, we devoted the rest of the session to explaining hypnosis to Molly. She was briefed in a way similar to the example given at the end of Chapter 1. At this time Molly was also told that she was expected to lose no more than two or three pounds a week. It was explained to her that the goal of treatment was a permanent weight loss that would need to be associated with an adjustment in body metabolism and a change in her eating and exercise patterns.

A second appointment was made for later in that week to begin the trance work. (Often the first two sessions can be combined in one double session; however, in this case both the patient's and therapist's busy schedules precluded that.) The second session began with the therapist's asking Molly if she had any questions about any of the things they had talked about previously. She said no, only that she was very anxious to begin.

She was asked to make herself comfortable. Then the trance work began by having Molly do some deep breathing and then focus her attention on different parts of her body, imagining how those parts felt and comparing how they felt when she inhaled to how they felt when she exhaled. She was then instructed to do a standard chalkboard instruction, in which she imagined numbers from 100 to zero on a chalkboard and counted them out loud, starting at 100 and finishing at zero. As she was doing this, the therapist engaged in hypnotic patter. When she got to zero, she was instructed to imagine herself at her favorite place and to deepen the experience by using all her sensory channels during that imagination process. Molly was then told that her only job was to continue using her imagination to enjoy her favorite place, while the therapist talked to her.

Next, I told a long, slow version of the roller coaster story (see Chapter 4) as a way of deepening the trance by repeating the embedded suggestion for her to "let go." I then gave her some early learning set messages, which suggested to her that there had been lots of times in her life when she had faced tasks that seemed difficult or almost impossible, and yet she overcame these so easily that she now forgets that at one time they were so difficult. She was reminded of when she learned to walk, when she learned the alphabet, when she first went in front of a TV camera, etc. She was then told the story about the friend (in this case, named Marion), who learned to say "no" to sexual advances and felt good about herself (see Chapter 4). Then the session ended by establishing an anchor, associating a grasp on her right shoulder with the feeling of being powerful and in control (see Chapter 3).

She was asked to alert herself, and was asked, "Molly, I'm just curious, how long did it seem to you, from the first time you closed your eyes until right now?" Molly thought for a minute and said, "Ten minutes, possibly 15 at the most, probably 10." I said, "Would you be surprised to know that it is closer to 45 minutes?" She was surprised and I explained to her that time distortion is a common phenomenon of trance. The only reason I explained this to Molly was that I knew that trance often seems like a very ordinary experience and that Molly might have believed that nothing really happened in this session. In fact, I wanted her to know that she was a very good subject, and had done extremely well for the first time. I wanted her to know that something unusual had occurred. She looked puzzled and yet somewhat delighted at the ratification of trance. She was told to begin on a diet that had previously worked for her, and was instructed to weigh herself only once a week, the morning of therapy.

The third session began one week later. Molly had lost four pounds and was feeling very good. She was cautioned to make sure that her diet felt comfortable and was not a deprivation diet. We then talked for a few minutes about exercise, which I explained was critical in order to successfully lose weight. Since she said she didn't mind exercising, except for the fact it was such a boring use of her time, it was suggested that she get an exercise bike, put it in her living room, and watch television or listen to the stereo while she was pedaling the bike. She felt this was a good idea and committed herself to getting a bike and doing the exercise.

Trance work was begun by repeating the induction from the previous session. Much of this session was a reminder of what had been said last session. There were also some direct suggestions about the good feeling she would have about herself as she continued to exert more and more willpower. She was then asked to imagine herself in the evening or on the weekend – times in the past when she used to have so much trouble – going into her kitchen to get food that she didn't need. As she gave a signal to say that she imagined herself in the kitchen, she was told to say to herself, "No I don't need that!" At the time she was saying this to herself, the power anchor on her right shoulder was fired, associating the feelings of power with the statement, "No, I don't need that!"

By the beginning of the fourth session, Molly had lost eleven and a half pounds and was feeling good about that, but beginning to feel "shaky" about her ability to keep the weight off. She talked about having more urges this past week than the previous two to "break her diet and pig out."

This session was scheduled for two hours, in order to do a reframing. The session followed the steps of reframing as described in Chapter 6. During the course of this treatment it was discovered that Molly's two main secondary gains for continuing to overeat and be overweight were 1) to avoid men, whom she found very scary since her divorce, and 2) to reduce stress in her life, especially during times of pressure in her work situation. The alternative behaviors that were generated were as follows: First, Molly, who was instructed about self-hypnosis after the third session, would continue to do self-hypnosis not only at night but also during every lunchtime on work days. This was a time when she was very tired, after having worked all morning and doing the noon news, and yet it preceded a busy and demanding time in terms of preparing things for the evening and the next day. She agreed that, no matter how busy she was, she would take 20 minutes for herself and do self-hypnosis every day.

In terms of dealing with men, two alternatives were generated. The first, which was based on a new insight that she became aware of during trance, was that she could still say "no" to men sexually even if she had a perfect figure. She realized that she did not need to be overweight as a way to keep men at a distance. She saw herself as an independent woman and realized that another way of asserting her independence was by just consciously choosing to say "no," rather than hiding behind excess weight. More importantly, she realized that she didn't really want to say "no" all the time, and that she needed to work on some unresolved issues around her divorce and the subsequent negative feelings generalized to all men. She contracted to see me for as many weeks as necessary in traditional talking therapy to deal with her issues involving men. So, once again, she decided to do much more self-hypnosis to help with stress reduction (she was finding it enjoyable anyway), and she planned to deal with men by temporarily saying "no," but having the goal of working in therapy on the problems she was having around sex.

I saw Molly seven times during the next ten weeks. Most of these sessions were spent in more traditionally oriented therapy, helping her resolve some of the leftover issues from her marital breakup. She was encouraged to begin dating in more intimate ways some of the men that she liked but had previously kept at arm's length. During this time, we did a half-session's worth of trance on four occasions, doing a little bit of anchoring with some direct and indirect suggestions. These were presented to her as "booster shots." Over this time, Molly was able to lose 19 pounds, and subsequently, during the next three months, she was able to stabilize this loss and lose four more pounds on her own. She was doing self-hypnosis about three nights and four days a week, was exercising regularly, was dating, and generally enjoying life.

This case illustrates the not uncommon situation of a person coming in specifically for hypnosis for habit control, but discovering in the process some issues that need to be addressed in a more traditional therapeutic way. This is why we emphasize, over and over again, that people doing this type of work should be trained in psychotherapy. An individual whose knowledge is limited to hypnosis is unable to adequately treat these problems.

TIM – ALCOHOLISM

Tim was a bright, 33-year-old man who was living with a young woman named Mary and their infant son, Joseph. Tim had two years of college and owned a successful dry cleaning business. He had separated three years earlier from Ellen after an eight-year marriage. He stated that, although he and Ellen had been very close emotionally, they were incompatible and argued a lot. While he was still living with Ellen, Tim met Mary and, after a yearlong affair, he separated from his wife. However, he still saw his wife occasionally but without Mary's knowledge.

When he called for an appointment, Tim stated that he wanted hypnotic treatment for interpersonal problems and to "get my life straightened out." He refused to bring anyone else, like his wife or girlfriend, into treatment with him. Tim was very confused and upset about the two women in his life and his child. His wife was pressuring him to return to the marriage. His girlfriend was insisting that he get a divorce and marry her. Tim stated that he wanted to be closer to his son Joseph, but just couldn't be until he knew what was going to be happening. Tim felt very hurt, guilty, and anxious about his situation.

He reported that he was drinking 4 to 12 beers daily and on occasion more, and was increasingly spending more time away from his business. Tim said he had been drinking beer since his mid-teens. He admitted that he was a heavy drinker but was defensive about the label "alcoholic." He had never been treated in the past for alcoholism or any other emotional problems.

At our first session, I took Tim's history and spent time getting into pace with him. I smelled the faint odor of alcohol on Tim's breath and told him I would not see him, but would still charge him for the session, if there was ever evidence of alcohol consumption prior to any future sessions. I told him that I would help him to straighten out his life, but that he would first have to stop drinking and maintain sobriety. I discussed the common observation that people are much more able to effectively deal with problems when drinking ceases. Tim admitted that he was running away from confronting his problems and that he had been "drowning his sorrows" with beer. Tim stated that he had stopped drinking many times before and insisted that he could do that again by himself. He agreed to a commitment to maintain sobriety for six months.

When I had asked Tim to identify some of the matters that he had been neglecting, he mentioned the books and records for his dry cleaning business. Therefore, before our first session ended, I gave him the directive to "straighten out" the business records by our next session. This, of course, was a metaphorical directive which related to Tim's life.

At the second session one week later, Tim reported that he had been sober since our first session and that he had straightened things out at work. He felt good about that and more optimistic about getting his personal life in order. He also said that he had thought about our discussion a week earlier and decided that he probably was an alcoholic. I then asked Tim to attend two AA meetings in different locations and with different groups of people in the following week, and he reluctantly agreed to do that. Tim explained that he prided himself on doing things on his own, and that even coming to me for help was unique for him.

At that second session, I discussed trance and hypnosis with Tim and induced trance using a structured induction (imagining taking an elevator from the tenth to the first floor and stepping out to his "favorite place") followed by conversational patter. While he was in trance, I made direct suggestions to Tim to do self-hypnosis twice daily by using the elevator induction. I also indirectly set up therapeutic potentials (to help him make decisions regarding his interpersonal life) by talking about the stock market (in which Tim was interested, so it was a pace for him) and how it sometimes was important to "hold onto" a stock and sometimes important to "let it go" and invest the resources elsewhere, and that often such decisions were difficult to make.

Our third session was 10 days later. Although he reported being very tempted to drink, Tim had maintained sobriety, had gone into trance regularly with success, and had attended the AA meetings. He complained about attending AA, however, and insisted he could maintain sobriety without it. At that session, I began a reframing (Chapter 6) with Tim which was not completed until our fourth session a week later. Tim became aware that the unconscious part of him responsible for drinking had been feeling "afraid of growing up and all its responsibilities" and "just wanted for him to have a good time." The main payoffs from drinking were self-tranquilization of hurt and guilt he felt about his wife and girlfriend and avoidance of responsibilities related to his making decisions about his personal life. As alternatives, Tim decided to continue to use self-hypnosis to comfort or tranquilize himself and to make the decisions he had to make so he and others could go on with their lives. During reframing, I utilized an anchor for power to help Tim say "no" to alcohol within relevant future contexts (e.g., lunchtime at work, after work, watching football on TV).

At our fifth session two weeks later, Tim told me that he had still been sober, that he was doing self-hypnosis regularly, and that he was routinely putting in a full day's work at his business. He said that he discovered that he could now just go into trance spontaneously and therefore no longer needed the elevator induction. At that session, Tim also informed me that he had decided to tell his wife, Ellen, that he wanted to get a divorce. He said that he felt in love with Mary, that he had been spending more time with Joseph and felt closer to him, and he wanted to go on with his life. Tim said he felt very anxious about telling Ellen of his decision and asked for my help. During trance, I let him imagine talking to Ellen as I fired the power anchor that had been established earlier (Chapter 3). Several days later, he told Ellen of his decision.

Our sixth session two weeks later was uneventful. At the seventh session two weeks after that, Tim remorsefully told me that he had gotten drunk the prior weekend. He said that an old drinking buddy, unaware that Tim was maintaining sobriety, had come by the shop on Friday and suggested that they have a few beers. Tim said he wanted to reward himself for the positive things he had been doing and prove to himself that he could drink two or three beers and then stop. Instead, he drank about 15 beers and came home at three in the morning. The following day he felt very guilty about his actions, and Mary was upset with him because he had gotten drunk and stayed out so late. Tim's way of dealing with the situation was to get drunk again that night. Tim and I discussed all these events with an orientation toward what he could learn from it all. Part of our discussion involved my explaining to Tim how his drinking over the weekend illustrated the "loss of control" phenomenon often displayed in alcoholism. As a result of his relapse, Tim expressed a more sincere conviction that, indeed, he was an alcoholic and needed to abstain from alcohol.

In retrospect, I decided that I should have realized that Tim's treatment had been proceeding almost "too smoothly" and that I *might* have been able to short-circuit the relapse in some way. I may have been able to utilize some indirect communication techniques discussed in Chapter 4. For example, I could have mentioned the disastrous results that occurred when other patients who were progressing satisfactorily had begun to believe that they could drink in a controlled manner.

At my request, Tim agreed to bring his girlfriend Mary to our next session. He also agreed to attend AA again. I told him that his active participation in AA would help me to feel more comfortable in reducing our treatment sessions and eventually terminating treatment.

At our eighth session nine days later, Tim came with Mary

and reported that he had attended three AA meetings. He also stated that he felt more comfortable about actively participating in that program. Tim, Mary and I discussed their relationship and Tim's alcoholism. Much of the focus was on how the two of them could have handled the situation more positively when Tim had gotten drunk several weeks earlier. I suggested to Mary that she participate in Alanon (for family members of alcoholics) and she agreed.

At our ninth session two weeks later, Tim and I discussed what was happening in his life and did hypnotic work. In general, the trance work was oriented toward reinforcing the positive gains Tim had achieved and suggesting even more power and control on his part. Tim had maintained sobriety since his relapse, was doing self-hypnosis regularly, and was attending an average of three AA meetings weekly. Mary was attending one Alanon meeting weekly and the two were getting along very well.

Two weeks later, at our tenth session, Tim told me that Mary had been asking when they would get married. He told her in six months and she agreed. However, when I asked him for his rationale for the six-month wait, he had none and it was clear that this reflected his tendency to avoid getting on with his life. On his own, Tim decided to surprise Mary with his new decision to get married sooner and the event took place three weeks later.

I continued to see Tim on a steadily decreasing basis until we finally terminated our therapeutic relationship at our fourteenth session. Although Mary had stopped attending Alanon, Tim was continuing to actively participate in AA. Part of the last session with Tim was spent doing trance work, during which time I thanked Tim and especially his unconscious and suggested that his growth continue. Here is a transcript of some of that communication:

> Tim, I know you don't need my thanks but I do want to thank you and all parts of you, especially your unconscious mind for the communication and for all the nice things that you've been doing for yourself. Everything that you've experienced here will be

there in your unconscious even though your conscious mind may forget. But your unconscious mind will let your conscious mind remember whatever is important whenever that might be helpful for you. I'd like to suggest that you may have learned much more than your conscious mind realizes and that all that learning is going to help you out as time goes on. You might wonder just how much and in just how many ways it will come in handy for you.

About six months after terminating my treatment with Tim, I received a note from him informing me that he had just celebrated his one year anniversary of sobriety. He was actively participating in AA, had opened up another dry cleaning shop, and looked forward with Mary to the birth of their second child.

CHAPTER 10

THE TRUTH

IN CHAPTER 1 we told you that we know of no truths, only our own realities. Maybe that was just one of our well-known "therapeutic fictions."

Since you have read this far you may be curious to know that collectively we have four biological children, four stepchildren, and more on the way. As fathers we want some real truths to teach our children. So here are the five givens in life!

When in doubt, go ahead.

Hold on tight and don't drag your feet.

If you have an itch, scratch it.

You're never too old to sit on your daddy's lap.

Never write the end of a book when the moon is full.

You may wonder if we really believe these to be the important truths of life. You may well wonder!

REFERENCES AND BIBLIOGRAPHY

Araoz, D. (1982). *Hypnosis and sex therapy*. New York: Brunner/Mazel.

Bach, R. (1977). *Illusions*. New York: Dell.

Bandler, R., & Grinder, J. (1975). *The structure of magic* (Vol. I). Palo Alto, CA: Science and Behavior Books.

Bandler, R., & Grinder, J. (1982). *Frogs into princes*. Moab, UT: Real People Press.

Bandler, R., & Grinder, J. (1982). *Reframing: Neuro-linguistic programming and the transformation of meaning*. Moab, UT: Real People Press.

Bandler, R., Grinder, J., & Satir, V. (1976). *Changing with families*. Palo Alto, CA: Science and Behavior Books.

Barber, J. (1980). Hypnosis and the unhypnotizable. *American Journal of Clinical Hypnosis, 23* (1).

Barber, J., & Adrian, C. (Eds.) (1982). *Psychological approaches to the management of pain*. New York: Brunner/Mazel.

Bateson, G. (1972). *Steps to an ecology of mind*. New York: Ballantine Books.

Bateson, G. (1979). *Mind and nature: A necessary unity*. New York: Dutton.

Bettelheim, B. (1975). *The uses of enchantment*. New York: Random House.

Cameron-Bandler, L. (1978). *They lived happily ever after*. Cupertino, CA: Meta Publications.

Conrad, P., & Schneider, J. (1980). *Deviance and medicalization: From badness to sickness*. St. Louis: C. V. Mosby.

Dilts, R., Grinder, J., Bandler, R., Bandler, L., & DeLozier, J. (1980). *Neuro-linguistic programming: The study of the structure of subjective experience* (Vol. I). Cupertino, CA: Meta Publications.

Erickson, M. H. (1980). *The collected papers of Milton H. Erickson on hypnosis* (4 vols.). Ernest L. Rossi (Ed.). New York: Irvington.

Erickson, M. H. (1983). *Healing in hypnosis*. New York: Irvington.

Erickson, M. H., Hershman, S., & Secter, I. (1981). *The practical ap-

plication of medical and dental hypnosis. Chicago: Seminars of Hypnosis.

Erickson, M. H., & Rossi, E. L. (1979). *Hypnotherapy: An exploratory casebook*. New York: Irvington.

Erickson, M. H., & Rossi, E. L. (1980). *Experiencing hypnosis*. New York: Irvington.

Erickson, M. H., Rossi, E. L., & Rossi, S. I. (1976). *Hypnotic realities: The induction of clinical hypnosis and forms of indirect suggestion*. New York: Irvington.

Farrelly, F., & Brandsma, J. (1974). *Provocative therapy*. Cupertino, CA: Meta Publications.

Fisch, R., Weakland, J., & Segal, L. (1982). *The tactics of change: Doing therapy briefly*. San Francisco, CA: Jossey-Bass.

Fromm, E., & Shor, R. (1979). *Hypnosis: Developments in research and new perspectives*. New York: Aldine.

Gardner, G., & Olness, K. (1981). *Hypnosis and hypnotherapy with children*. New York: Grune and Stratton.

Gilman, A. G., Goodman, L., & Gilman, A. (Eds.) (1980). *Goodman and Gilman's the pharmacological basis of therapeutics* (6th ed.). New York: Macmillan.

Goodheart, R. & Shils, M. (1980). *Modern nutrition in health and disease* (6th ed.). Philadelphia: Lea and Ferbiger.

Gordon, D. (1978). *Therapeutic metaphors*. Cupertino, CA: Meta Publications.

Gordon, D., & Meyers-Anderson, M. (1981). *Phoenix: Therapeutic patterns of Milton H. Erickson*. Cupertino, CA: Meta Publications.

Grinder, J., & Bandler, R. (1981). *Trance-formations: Neurolinguistic programming and the structure of hypnosis*. Moab, UT: Real People Press.

Grinder, J., DeLozier, J., & Bandler, R. (1977). *Patterns of the hypnotic techniques of Milton H. Erickson, M.D.* (Vol. II). Cupertino, CA: Meta Publications.

Haley, J. (1963). *Strategies of psychotherapy*. New York: Grune and Stratton.

Haley, J. (Ed.) (1967). *Advanced techniques of hypnosis and therapy: Selected papers of Milton H. Erickson, M.D.* New York: Grune and Stratton.

Haley, J. (1973). *Uncommon therapy: The psychiatric techniques of Milton H. Erickson, M.D.* New York: Norton.

Haley, J. (1976). *Problem solving therapy*. New York: Harper and Row.

Haley, J. (1984). *Ordeal therapy*. San Francisco, CA: Jossey-Bass.

Hoffman, L. (1981). *Foundations of family therapy*. New York: Basic Books.

Hofman, F. (1983). *A handbook on drug and alcohol abuse: The biomedical aspects* (2nd ed.). New York: Oxford University Press.

Jaffe, J. H. (1980). *Drug addiction and drug abuse.* In A. G. Gilman, L. Goodman & A. Gilman (Eds.), *Goodman and Gilman's the pharmacological basis of therapeutics.* (6th ed.). New York: Macmillan.

Jaffe, J., Peterson, R., & Hodgson, R. (1979). *Addictions: Issues and answers.* New York: Harper and Row.

Jellinek, E. (1960). *Disease concept of alcoholism.* New Haven: United Printing Service.

King, M., Novik, L., & Citrenbaum, C. (1983). *Irresistible communication: Creative skills for the health professional.* Philadelphia: W. B. Saunders.

Kroger, W. S. & Fezler, W. D. (1976). *Hypnosis and behavior modification: Imagery conditioning.* Philadelphia: Lippincott.

Lankton, S. R., & Lankton, C. H. (1983). *The answer within: A clinical framework of Ericksonian hypnotherapy.* New York: Brunner/Mazel.

Lustig, H. (1975). *The artistry of Milton H. Erickson, M.D.* (Part I and II) [Videotape]. Haverford, PA: Herbert S. Lustig, M.D., Ltd.

Nietzsche, F. (1968a). Letters. In W. Kaufman (Trans.), *The portable Nietzsche.* Princeton: Princeton University Press.

Nietzsche, F. (1968b). Twilight of the idols. In W. Kaufman (Trans.), *The portable Nietzsche.* Princeton: Princeton University Press.

Rosen, S. (1982). *My voice will go with you: The teaching tales of Milton H. Erickson.* New York: Norton.

Springer, S., & Deutsch, G. (1981). *Left brain, right brain.* San Francisco: Freeman.

Steiner, C. (1971). *Games alcoholics play.* New York: Grove Press.

Stolzenberg, G. (1984). Can an inquiry into the foundations of mathematics tell us anything interesting about mind? In P. Watzlawick (Ed.), *The invented reality.* New York: Norton.

Teitelbaum, M. (1965). *Hypnosis induction techniques.* Springfield, IL: Charles C. Thomas.

Valle, R., & King, M. (1978). *Existential-phenomenological alternatives for psychology.* New York: Oxford University Press.

Watzlawick, P. (1976). *How real is real?* New York: Random House.

Watzlawick, P. (1978). *The language of change.* New York: Basic Books.

Watzlawick, P. (1983). *The situation is hopeless, but not serious: The pursuit of unhappiness.* New York: Norton.

Watzlawick, P. (1985). Hypnotherapy without trance. In J. K. Zeig (Ed.), *Ericksonian psychotherapy. Volume 1: Structures.* New York: Brunner/Mazel.

Watzlawick, P., Beavin, J., & Jackson, D. (1967). *Pragmatics of human communication.* New York: Norton.

Watzlawick, P., Weakland, J., & Fisch, R. (1974). *Change: Principles of problem formation and problem resolution.* New York: Norton.

Weeks, G., & L'Abate, L. (1982). *Paradoxical psychotherapy: Theory and practice with individuals, couples, and families.* New York: Brunner/Mazel.

Weitzenhoffer, A. (1980). Hypnotic susceptibility revisited. *American Journal of Clinical Hypnosis, 22* (3).

Whitfield, C., Thompson, G., Lamb, A., Spencer, V., Pfiefer, M., & Browning-Ferrando, M. (1978). Detoxification of 1,024 alcoholic patients without psychoactive drugs. *Journal of the American Medical Association, 239* (14), 1409-10.

Yapko, M. (1983). A comparative analysis of direct and indirect hypnotic communication styles. *American Journal of Clinical Hypnosis, 24:* 270-276.

Zeig, J. (Ed.) (1980). *A teaching seminar with Milton H. Erickson, M.D.* New York: Brunner/Mazel.

Zeig, J. (Ed.) (1982). *Ericksonian approaches to hypnosis and psychotherapy.* New York: Brunner/Mazel.

INDEX